D1338912

dirigenten der ddr

*conductors of the german
democratic republic*

*otmar suitner
herbert kegel
heinz rögner
heinz bongartz
helmut koch*

*discographies compiled
by john hunt*

4

Contents

Published 2010 John Hunt.

© 2010 John Hunt

ISBN: 978-1-901395-25-9

Sole distributors:
Travis & Emery
17 Cecil Court
London, WC2N 4EZ
United Kingdom.
Tel. (+44) 20 7 240 2129

Dirigenten der DDR: an introduction

Greater Germany's leading position in the field of classical music was undisputed throughout Europe during the first half of the twentieth century. This was not least due to the fact that so many of the major composers and performers originated out of a German background, and that traditions were unswervingly upheld and respected. Even in the darker years of the Third Reich, the defection of a few dozen of the country's top performers (conductors, singers and instrumentalists) did little to debilitate the solid basis on which music, and its dissemination through radio broadcasts and through recordings, rested. Indeed, it is the importance which various totalitarian regimes attached to the media as a means of communication that we have to thank for the survival of so many recordings of notable musical events from the 1930s onwards.

Notwithstanding the fact that Germany's defeat at the end of World War II was the result of its own mistakes, it nevertheless had the most serious implications on many levels, not least for the administration of cultural matters and musical practice in particular. The ensuing partition between East (Soviet occupation) and West (Allied Powers occupation), neither of whose powers possessed any specialist knowledge of Germany's musical past, left considerable scope for improvisation. And although they may not have fully realised it in the earliest post war years, the Soviet occupiers held the greatest musical treasures in the palm of their hands, with renowned orchestras in Berlin (apart from the Berlin Philharmonic itself), Dresden and Leipzig. They also encompassed in their territory the birthplaces of many a musical luminary – Bach, Handel, Weber, Mendelssohn, Schumann, Wagner and so on.

As far as the very highest level of conducting talent was concerned, things were more difficult. Wilhelm Furtwängler, after conducting initial performances of *Tristan* for the Berlin Staatsoper in the autumn of 1947, could not be persuaded to enter into a permanent relationship with the institution where he had in happier times held such an honoured position. Erich Kleiber also ended a short courtship with the Soviet authorities on the very eve of re-opening the rebuilt Staatsoper building. In quick succession, the other representatives of the old German tradition who had chosen the newly constituted DDR as the field of their activities, both died (Hermann Abendroth in 1956 and Franz Konwitschny in 1962).

The path was now open for new figures to emerge, but mainly because of decreasing cordial relations between East and West the new DDR conductors, some of whom form the basis for this discography, had few opportunities to take guest-conducting engagements in the West. The result was comparative obscurity for them outside of the record catalogues, which is the main reason why I have preceeded each discography with a brief biographical sketch. One important characteristic of Otmar Suitner and the other conductors in our group was loyalty to the institution: loyalty is nowadays as outmoded a concept as tradition itself, yet its importance in consolidating the musical achievement of the DDR can now be appreciated at face value, regardless of whether we condone or vilify the political regime.

Without wishing to decry the highly professional qualities of the various West German radio orchestras which proliferated in the postwar years, it fell to their counterparts in Leipzig and Berlin (Rundfunk-Sinfonie-Orchester Leipzig and Rundfunk-Sinfonie-Orchester Berlin, the latter having been founded back in 1925) to reflect the characteristic middle European sound quality of the more well-known Staatskapelle Berlin, Gewandhaus-Orchester Leipzig and Sächsische Staatskapelle Dresden. The sound of all the orchestras in these discographies is a far cry from those in our own materialistic age, which has contributed to bringing about a uniformity in orchestral sound, with most individual qualities erased in the pursuit of abstract perfection. This was a fact which I was lamenting a decade ago in my discography of the Wiener Philharmoniker: my experience is that by today's reckoning only the Sächsische Staatskapelle Dresden and the Concertgebouworkest Amsterdam still retain a real individualism in their performances: the rest simply strive for faceless American-style perfectionism !

The vintage East German sound was of course abetted by recording technology and acoustics of an unparalled distinction. The state-run Eterna recording company had at its disposal studios set up in the Christuskirche in Berlin-Oberschönerweide (not to be confused with the Jesus-Christus-Kirche in Berlin-Dahlem used by Western recording companies), the Lukaskirche in Dresden and three main venues in Leipzig: Kongresshalle, Versöhnungskirche and Paul-Gerhardt-Kirche. In addition, there was access in Berlin and Leipzig to the facilities of the state-controlled Radio DDR, with an especially fine and mellow acoustic to be heard in the Berlin studios in the Napaletastrasse even into the last decade of the century: some of Daniel Barenboim's first recordings with the Staatskapelle Berlin were apparently still made there!

A highly practical six-digit numbering system was employed by Eterna
for its discs, which can be summarised as follows:

78rpm shellac discs	110 000/120 000/121 000/130 000/
	140 000/150 000/320 000/340 000
45rpm microgroove discs	410 000/450 000/510 000/520 000/
	530 000/540 000/550 000/560 000
33rpm 10-inch mono lp	710 000/720 000/750 000/760 000
33rpm 12-inch mono lp	810 000/820 000/821 000/822 000/
	830 000/840 000/860 000
33rpm 12-inch stereo lp	825 000/826 000/827 000/725 000/
	728 000/729 000
Compact discs	329 000

*Separate lp categories existed for lighter music (amiga 845 000) and contemporary
music (nova 885 000)*

For help with these discographies I am grateful to Michael H. Gray
(who enabled me to view an almost complete inventory of Eterna's
production}, Graham Silcock (whose two-part article *The musical legacy
of a vanished land* appeared in the spring and summer 1997 editions of
Classic Record Collector, yielding much useful background information),
Yasushi Aisa, John Baker, John Hancock, Roderick Krüsemann,
Anton Schwab and my good friend Klaus Heinze, former member of
the Sächsische Staatskapelle Dresden. In addition, just before going to
press I had the good fortune to meet another representative of DDR
music-making, the soprano Jutta Vulpius, who was able to recall for me
specific recordings in which she had participated. I do however stress
that the opinions expressed in this introduction are mine alone, as are
any errors which may have crept into the discographies themselves.

Abbreviations are kept to a minimum, in fact only RSOB (Rundfunk-
Sinfonie-Orchester-Berlin) and RSOL (Rundfunk-Sinfonie-Orchester-
Leipzig, nowadays known as MDR-Sinfonie-Orchester) are used.
Soloists participating in the recordings are listed by surname only
immediately after the orchestra details, but a separate index at the end
of the book gives full names, wherever this is possible, for
identification purposes.

John Hunt Copyright 2010

8
Bibliography

VEB Deutsche Schallplatten/*Hauptkatalog 1958*

Eterna/*Hauptkatalog 1970*

Händel-Jahrbuch 1978/*Herausgegeben von der G-F-Händel-Gesellschaft VEB Deutscher Verlag für Musik Leipzig*

John L. Holmes: Conductors on Record/*Gollancz 1982*

125 Jahre Dresdner Philharmonie
DZA Verlag für Kultur und Wissenschaft 1995

Klangbilder: Portrait der Staatskapelle Berlin
Herausgegeben von Georg Quander/Propyläen Verlag 1995

Sächsische Staatskapelle Dresden 1923-1998
Discographie vorgelegt von Klaus Heinze 1998

Anny Schlemm: Stimmen, die um die Welt gingen
Herausgegeben von Günter Walter 1998-2000

Sächsische Staatskapelle Dresden 1911-2001
Discography compiled by John Hunt 2002

Meine herrliche Kapelle: Otmar Suitner und die Staatskapelle Berlin
Herausgegeben von Dirk Stöve/Henschel Verlag 2002

Ernst Kozub: Stimmen, die um die Welt gingen
Herausgegeben von Günter Walter 2002

Herbert Kegel: Ein Dirigentenleben im 20. Jahrhundert
Herausgegeben von Helga Kuschmitz/Verlag Klaus-Jürgen Kamprad 2003

Karsten Steiger: Operndiskographie 2. Ausgabe
Saur Verlag 2008

Dirigenten der DDR: Einführung in die Diskographie

In der ersten Hälfte des zwanzigsten Jahrhunderts hielt Grossdeutschland im klassischen Musikbereich eine führende Stellung inne. Nicht zumindest war das der Tatsache zu verdanken, dass so viele der Künstler, schaffende sowie nachschaffende, deutscher Herkunft waren und dass ihre Traditionen aufrechterhalten wurden. Selbst die Auswanderungen der dunklen Nazijahre, wo ein paar Dutzend der namhaftesten Dirigenten, Sänger und Instrumentalisten ihre Heimat verliessen, haben die solide Grundlage des Musikbetriebs und deren Verbreitung durch Rundfunk und Schallplatte kaum geschwächt. Eigentlich haben wir mehreren totalitären Machthabern es zu verdanken, dass sie in ihrer Medienbewusstheit dazu beigetragen haben, so viele wichtige musikalische Ereignisse schon ab den dreissiger Jahren aufgenommen und aufbewahrt zu haben.

Obwohl Deutschlands Niederlage 1945 unleugbare Folge der eigenen Fehler war, so hat sie sich doch auf zahllose Bereiche ausgewirkt, nicht zuletzt im Kulturbereich und in der Musikpraxis insbesonders. Die nachfolgende Teilung des Landes zwischen Ost (Sowjets) und West (Alliierten), deren Bezatzungsmächte keine präzisen Kenntnisse der musikalischen Vergangenheit besassen, liess freien Raum für Verbesserung. Vielleicht haben die Sowjets in den frühen Nachkriegsjahren nicht völlig zur Kenntnis genommen, dass sie die grössten musikalischen Schätze in ihren Händen hielten, mit renommierten Klangkörpern in Berlin (ausser Philharmonisches Orchester), Dresden und Leipzig, sowie die Geburtsorte mancher bedeutender Persönlichkeit – Bach, Händel, Weber, Mendelssohn, Schumann, Wagner usw.

Was dem höchsten Rang der Dirigierkunst betrifft, liefen die Dinge etwas schwieriger. Wilhelm Furtwängler wollte sich, nach einer erfolgreichen Tristan-Reihe in der Berliner Staatsoper im Herbst 1947, in kein dauerndes Arbeitsverhältnis mit dem ihm in glücklicheren Zeiten so verbundenen Institut hineinreden lassen. Erich Kleiber brach nach kurzer Werbung mit den sowjetischen Behörden eine Bindung mit dem selben Haus jäh ab – sogar am Vorabend der Wiedereröffnung des wiederaufgebauten Theaters ! Kurz danach schieden aus dem Leben die beiden anderen Vertreter der älteren deutschen Dirigiertradition, die die neugegründete DDR als ihre Wirkungsstätte auserwählt hatten: Hermann Abendroth starb 1956, Franz Konwitschny 1962.

Für neue Kräfte war der Weg nun frei, doch aufgrund der immer
schlechter werdenden Verhältnisse zwischen Ost und West hatten die
neueren DDR-Dirigenten, die in dieser Diskographie behandelt werden,
wenige Gelegenheiten, im Westen aufzutreten. Sie blieben also
ausserhalb der Zonengrenze verhältnismässig unbekannt, was mich
hier veranlasst, den einzelnen Diskographien eine kurze biographische
Skizze voranstellen zu lassen. Die zu betonende Eigenschaft von
Otmar Suitner und seinen Kollegen ist unbestreitbar ihre Treue zum
Institut: Treue ist heutzutage ein so abgewertetes Konzept wie die
Tradition selber, doch kann ihr Beitrag zu musikalischen Leistungen
in der DDR kaum widersprochen werden, egal ob wir das politische
Regime gutheissen oder verabscheuen.

Ohne die hohen Leistungen der in der Bundesrepublik entstandenen
Rundfunkorchester unterschätzen zu wollen, fiel es ihren Kollegen
in Leipzig und Berlin (Rundfunk-Sinfonie-Orchester Leipzig und
Rundfunk-Sinfonie-Orchester Berlin, dieses schon in den zwanziger
Jahren gegründet), zur Aufgabe, jenen typischen mitteleuropäischen
(soliden und warmen) Klang zu bewahren, so wie er in den
etabliertesten Klangkörpern (Staatskapelle Berlin, Leipziger Gewandhaus-
Orchester und Sächsische Staatskapelle Dresden) schon längst gebettet
war. Was wir beim Anhören der in diesem Buch gelisteten
Schallaufnahmen erleben, ist weit davon entfernt, was wir heutzutage
in unserem höchst materialistischen Zeitalter von unseren Orchestern
zu Ohren geboten werden: individuelle Klangeigenschaften werden
zugunsten einer unpersönlichen Glätte unterdrückt, eine Entwicklung,
die ich schon vor einem Jahrzehnt in meiner Diskographie der
Wiener Philharmoniker beklagte. Meines Erachtens behalten für uns
heute nur noch die Orchester in Dresden und Amsterdam (Sächsische
Staatskapelle und Concertgebouworkest) ihren ortsbestimmten
Individualismus, alle anderen streben dem gesichtslosen
Perfektionismus nach amerikanischem Muster entgegen.

Der altbewährte Ostklang wurde dagegen bis in die achtziger Jahre teils
durch eine unvergleichliche Aufnahmetechnik und von hohen
akustischen Verhältnissen geprägt. Dem volkseigenen Betrieb Deutsche
Schallplatten, später und besser als Eterna bekannt, standen
Aufnahmeorte wie die Christuskirche in Berlin-Oberschöneweide
(nicht zu verwechseln mit der Jesus-Christus-Kirche im westlichen
Berlin-Dahlem), Lukaskirche Dresden und die drei Leipziger Hallen,
Kongresshalle, Versöhnungskirche und Paul-Gerhard-Kirche zur
Verfügung. Noch dazu die Berliner und Leipziger Studiosäle des
Radio DDR, mit der besonders weichen und sanften Akustik des
Funkhauses in der Ostberliner Nalepastrasse: immer noch zu Ende

der neunziger Jahre entstanden hier Aufnahmen der Berliner
Staatskapelle unter Daniel Barenboim.

Ganz praktisch war das Numerierungssystem der Eterna-Platten :-

78UpM Schellack-Platten	110 000/120 000/121 000/130 000/ 140 000/150 000/320 000/340 000
45UpM 17cm Platten	410 000/450 000/510 000/520 000/ 530 000/540 000/550 000/560 000
33Upm 25cm Platten	710 000/720 000/750 000/760 000
33UpM 30cm Platten (mono)	810 000/820 000/821 000/822 000/ 830 000/840 000/860 000
33UpM 30cm Platten (stereo)	825 000/826 000/827 000/ 725 000/728 000/729 000
Compact discs	329 000

*Getrennte Kategorien galten für leichtere Musik (Amiga 845 000) und für
zeitgenössische Musik (885 000)*

Abkürzungen werden meistens vermieden, nur nicht bei RSOB
(Rundfunk-Sinfonie-Orchester Berlin) sowie bei RSOL (Rundfunk-
Sinfonie-Orchester Leipzig, heute bekannt als MDR Sinfonie-Orchester).
Instrumental- sowie Gesangssolisten werden direkt unter den
Orchesterangaben mit nur ihrem Familiennamen gekennzeichnet,
deshalb füge ich ein Künstlerverzeichnis mit vollen Namen am
Schluss der Diskographie bei.

Gedankt seien Michael H. Gray, der mir ein fast vollständiges Inventar
der Eterna-Produkrion zur Verfügung stellte, Graham Silcock, dessen
1997 in der Schallplattenzeitschrift *Classic Record Collector* erschienener
Beitrag *The musical legacy of a vanished land* mir viele positive Hinweise
gab, Yasushi Aisa, John Baker, John Hancock, Roderick
Krüsemann, Anton Schwab und mein guter Freund Klaus Heinze,
ehemaliges Mitglied der Sächsischen Staatskapelle Dresden. Kurz vor
Redaktionsschluss hatte ich noch dazu das Glück, mit der Sopranistin
Jutta Vulpius zusammenzutreffen, die sich an verschiedene Aufnahmen
erinnern konnte, an denen sie teilgenommen hatte. Es muss aber
betont werden, dass alle in diesem Textteil geäusserte Meinungen von
dem Verfasser stammen, der auch für irgendwelche in die Diskographien
eingeschlichene Fehler verantwortlich ist.

John Hunt 2010

Otmar Suitner 1922-2010

Born in Innsbruck and at one time rumoured to be related to the conductor Clemens Krauss, Suitner's first appointments were in Innsbruck, Remscheid and Ludwigshafen before taking on both opera and orchestral responsibilities in Dresden and, ultimately, East Berlin. However, for a number of seasons in the 1960s and 1970s, he did continue to appear in the West, both at the Bayreuth Festival and with the San Francisco Opera in the USA. Recordings surviving from those sources are also included in the discography.

Particularly outstanding in Suitner's discography are the Mozart series made with the Sächsische Staatskapelle Dresden, both the set of Symphonies 28-41 and operas *Die Entführung aus dem Serail*, *Le nozze di Figaro* and *Die Zauberflöte*. Symphonic cycles of Schubert, Beethoven, Brahms and Dvorak recorded later with the Berlin Staatskapelle have so far enjoyed less circulation internationally, but deserve closer scrutiny both for interpretation and for the flawless engineering carried out by Eterna in the Christuskirche.

LUDWIG VAN BEETHOVEN (1770-1827)
symphony no 1 in c op 21
recorded between 30 august-6 september 1983 in the christuskirche
staatskapelle berlin   lp: eterna 827 895
                                     cd: denon C37 7128/C37 7251-7256/
                                     CO 85063

symphony no 2 in d op 36
recorded on 5 march 1977 at a concert in the staatsoper
staatskapelle berlin   unpublished radio broadcast
                                     german radio archives

recorded between 12-19 june 1982 in the christuskirche
staatskapelle berlin   lp: eterna 827 785
                                     cd: denon C37 7367/C37 7251-7256/
                                     CO 85064/17001

symphony no 3 in e flat op 55 "eroica"
recorded on 22 march 1977 at a beethoven commemoration concert in the staatsoper
staatskapelle berlin   cd: weitblick (japan) SSS 05822

recorded on 23-25 june 1980 in the christuskirche
staatskapelle berlin   lp: eterna 827 489
                                     cd: denon C37 7011/C37 7251-7256/
                                     CO 85065/DC 8014

televised in 1981 at a concert in tokyo
nhk symphony   laserdisc: pioneer (japan)
                                     MC044-25NH

symphony no 4 in b flat op 60
recorded on 30 august-1 september 1983 in the christuskirche
staatskapelle berlin   lp: eterna 827 896
                                     cd: denon C37 7077/C37 7251-7256/
                                     CO 85066

14

beethoven/**symphony no 5 in c minor op 67**
recorded on 10-11 november 1968 in the funkhaus nalepastrasse
staatskapelle berlin   cd: pilz acanta 44 20552

televised on 7 june 1981 at a concert in yokohama
staatskapelle berlin   laserdisc: pioneer (japan)

recorded on 26-28 august 1981 in the christuskirche
staatskapelle berlin   lp: eterna 827 678
                              cd: denon C37 7001/C37 7251-7256/
                              CO 85064/17001

symphony no 6 in f op 68 "pastoral"
recorded on 1 july 1980 in the christuskirche
staatskapelle berlin   lp: eterna 827 526
                              cd: denon C37 7040/C37 7251-7256/
                              CO 85067
                              also published on cd by union square music

televised in 1980 at a concert in tokyo
nhk symphony   laserdisc: pioneer (japan)

symphony no 7 in a op 92
recorded on 29-31 august 1981 in the christuskirche
staatskapelle berlin   lp: eterna 827 650/827 895
                              cd: denon C37 7032/C37 7251-7256/
                              CO 85063
                              also published on cd by union square music

symphony no 8 in f op 93
recorded between 30 august-6 september 1983 in the christuskirche
staatskapelle berlin   lp: eterna 827 895
                              cd: denon C37 7128/C37 7251-7256/
                              CO 85066

beethoven/**symphony no 9 in d minor op 125 "choral"**
recorded between 12-19 june 1982 in the christuskirche

staatskapelle berlin	lp: eterna 827 788-789
rundfunkchor berlin	cd: denon C37 7021/C37 7251-7256/
hajossyova, priew,	CO 85068/17001
büchner, schenk	*choral movement also published on cd by union square music*

piano concerto no 1 in c op 15
recorded on 5 march 1977 at a concert in the staatsoper

staatskapelle berlin	unpublished radio broadcast
frieser	*german radio archives*

piano concerto no 4 in g op 58
recorded on 19-20 october 1987 in the abbey road studios london

london symphony	sony unpublished
nakamura	*produced by sony exclusively for the japanese market*

piano concerto no 5 in e flat op 73 "emperor"
recorded on 19-20 october 1987 in the abbey road studios london

london symphony	cd: sony 32DC 5021
nakamura	*produced by sony exclusively for the japanese market*

violin concerto in d op 61
recorded on 5 march 1987 at a concert in the schauspielhaus

staatskapelle berlin	unpublished radio broadcast
stadler	*german radio archives*

coriolan overture op 62
recorded between 17-20 september 1984 in the christuskirche

staatskapelle berlin	lp: eterna 725 045
	cd: denon C37 7367/CO 85065/
	DC 8014

egmont overture op 84
recorded between 17-20 september 1984 in the christuskirche

staatskapelle berlin	lp: eterna 725 045
	cd: denon C37 7367/CO 85065/
	DC 8014

beethoven/**fidelio overture op 72b**
recorded between 17-20 september 1984 in the christuskirche
staatskapelle berlin   lp: eterna 725 045
                              cd: denon C37 7367/CO 85067

abscheulicher wo eilst du hin?/fidelio
recorded in 1973 at a concert in stockholm
swedish radio   cd: opernwelt CD 2007
orchestra
ligendza

o welche lust, in freier luft den atem leicht zu heben!/fidelio
recorded in march 1977 and february 1978 in the christuskirche
staatskapelle berlin   lp: eterna 826 944/
chor der deutschen   deutsche schallplatten (japan) ET 5029
staatsoper   cd: berlin classics 83682
bindszus, riedel

die geschöpfe des prometheus overture op 43
recorded between 17-20 september 1984 in the christuskirche
staatskapelle berlin   lp: eterna 725 045

leonore no 3 overture op 72a
televised on 7 june 1981 at a concert in yokohama
staatskapelle berlin   laserdisc: pioneer (japan) MC044-25NH

recorded between 17-20 september 1984 in the christuskirche
staatskapelle berlin   lp: eterna 725 045
                              cd: denon C37 7367/CO 85067
                              also published on cd by union square music

die weihe des hauses overture op 124
recorded on 5 march 1977 at a concert in the staatsoper
staatskapelle berlin   cd: weitblick (japan) SSS 05822

ALBAN BERG (1885-1935)
violin concerto
recorded on 4 october 1985 at a concert in the schauspielhaus

staatskapelle berlin   unpublished radio broadcast
rezler   *german radio archives*

sieben frühe lieder
recorded on 12 june 1980 at a concert in the staatsoper

staatskapelle berlin   unpublished radio broadcast
davy   *german radio archives*

GUENTER BIALAS (1907-1995)
romanze für orchester
recorded on 17 january 1967 in the funkhaus nalepastrasse

staatskapelle berlin   unpublished radio broadcast
           german radio archives

GEORGES BIZET (1838-1875)
symphony in c
recorded in april 1972 in the lukaskirche

staatskapelle dresden   lp: eterna 826 342/eurodisc XK 86472/
           deutsche schallplatten (japan) ET 3003
           cd: berlin classics 02612/13582/32472/
           90402/93942

au fond du temple saint/les pecheurs de perles
recorded between 12-15 february 1972 in the lukaskirche

staatskapelle dresden   lp: eterna 826 334
schreier, adam   cd: berlin classics 20432
sung in german

JOHANNES BRAHMS (1833-1897)
symphony no 1 in c minor op 68
recorded on 1 october 1982 at a concert in the staatsoper
staatskapelle berlin   unpublished radio broadcast
         german radio archives

recorded on 4 october 1985 in the schauspielhaus
staatskapelle berlin   unpublished radio broadcast
         german radio archives

recorded in january 1986 in the christuskirche
staatskapelle berlin   lp: eterna 725 006
         cd: berlin classics 13502/21372

recorded on 13 june 1988 at a concert in tokyo
staatskapelle berlin   cd: altus (japan) ALT 024

symphony no 2 in d op 73
recorded berween 6-10 february 1984 in the christuskirche
staatskapelle berlin   lp: eterna 725 145
         cd: berlin classics 13502/21372

symphony no 3 in f op 90
recorded on 28-30 august 1985 in the christuskirche
staatskapelle berlin   lp: eterna 725 146
         cd: berlin classics 13502/21372

televised on 16 november 1989 at a concert in tokyo
nhk symphony   unpublished video recording
         rehearsal extracts also filmed

symphony no 4 in e minor op 98
recorded on 5 march 1965 at a concert in the staatsoper
staatskapelle berlin   unpublished radio broadcast
         german radio archives

recorded between 1-4 april 1986 in the christuskirche
staatskapelle berlin   lp: eterna 725 170
         cd: berlin classics 13502/21372

brahms/**violin concerto in d op 77**
recorded on 8 may 1987 at a concert in the schauspielhaus
staatskapelle berlin   unpublished radio broadcast
kagan   *german radio archives*

hungarian dances nos 1-21
recorded between 28 august-2 september 1989 in the christuskirche
staatskapelle berlin

REINER BREDEMEYER (1929-1995)
bagatellen für b, for piano and orchestra
recorded in 1979 in the christuskirche
staatskapelle berlin   lp: eterna 885 186
olbertz   cd: berlin classics 13032/wergo 62252

ANTON BRUCKNER (1824-1896)
symphony no 1 in c minor
recorded between 12-15 may 1987 in the christuskirche
staatskapelle berlin   cd: berlin classics 16326/deutsche
                              schallplatten (japan) TKCC 15011

symphony no 4 in e flat "romantic"
recorded between 10-14 october 1988 in the christuskirche
staatskapelle berlin   cd: berlin classics 13192/deutsche
                              schallplatten (japan) TKCC 15012

symphony no 5 in b flat
recorded between 8-13 january 1990 in the christuskirche
staatskapelle berlin   cd: berlin classics 02442/deutsche
                              schallplatten (japan) TKCC 15013

symphony no 7 in e flat
recorded between 23-27 january 1989 in the christuskirche
staatskapelle berlin   cd: berlin classics 83752/210 0212/
                              deutsche schallplatten (japan) TKCC 15014

bruckner/**symphony no 8 in c minor**
recorded on 9 september 1986 at a concert in the schauspielhaus
staatskapelle berlin   cd: weitblick (japan) SSS 03422

recorded in december 1986-january 1987 in the christuskirche
staatskapelle berlin   lp: eterna 729 171-172
                              cd: berlin classics 11632/deutsche
                              schallplatten (japan) TKCC 15015

CLAUDE DEBUSSY (1862-1918)
prelude a l'apres-midi d'un faune
recorded on 10-11 may 1962 in the lukaskirche
staatskapelle dresden   45: eterna 520 471
                               lp: eterna 720 172/825 984
                               cd: berlin classics 02612/30342

PAUL DESSAU (1894-1979)
orchestral music no 3 "lenin" for piano, childrens' choir, chorus
and orchestra
recorded on 14 october 1967 at a concert in the staatsoper
staatskapelle berlin   unpublished radio broadcast
rundfunkchor berlin   *german radio archives*
olbertz

recorded between 19-21 november 1975 in the christuskirche
staatskapelle berlin   lp: eterna 885 020
rundfunkchor berlin   cd: berlin classics 91822
olbertz

in memoriam bertholt brecht
recorded on 26 september 1975 at a concert in the staatsoper
staatskapelle berlin   unpublished radio broadcast
                              german radio archives

dessau/**einstein, opera in three acts**
recorded in 1977 in the funkhaus nalepastrasse

staatskapelle berlin	lp: eterna 885 102-104
chor der deutschen	cd: berlin classics 91092
staatsoper	
schreier, adam,	
leib, süss	

leonce und lena, opera in two acts
recorded in 1980 in the funkhaus nalepastrasse

staatskapelle berlin	lp: eterna 885 195
chor der deutschen	cd: berlin classics 10742
staatsoper	
nossek, eisenfeld,	
büchner, leib, süss	

ANTONIN DVORAK (1841-1904)
symphony no 1 in c minor "the bells of zlonice"
recorded between 27-30 august 1979 in the christuskirche

staatskapelle berlin   lp: eterna 827 424/deutsche
                              schallplatten (japan) ET 5088
                              cd: berlin classics 02782/92822/deutsche
                              schallplatten (japan) TKCC 70281

symphony no 2 in b flat op 4
recorded between 23-25 october 1979 in the christuskirche

staatskapelle berlin   lp: eterna 827 425/deutsche
                              schallplatten (japan) ET 5104
                              cd: berlin classics 02782/92822/deutsche
                              schallplatten (japan) TKCC 70282

symphony no 3 in e flat op 10
recorded between 5-9 july 1978 in the christuskirche

staatskapelle berlin   lp: eterna 827 292/deutsche
                              schallplatten (japan) ET 5087
                              cd: berlin classics 02782/92822/deutsche
                              schallplatten (japan) TKCC 70283

dvorak/**symphony no 4 in d minor op 13**
recorded between 15-19 december 1980 in the christuskirche

staatskapelle berlin	lp: eterna 827 539/deutsche schallplatten (japan) ET 5129
	cd: berlin classics 02442/02782/deutsche schallplatten (japan) TKCC 70283
	recording completed in february 1981

symphony no 5 in f op 24
recorded between 25-28 november 1977 in the christuskirche

staatskapelle berlin	lp: eterna 827 195/deutsche schallplatten (japan) ET 5050
	cd: berlin classics 02442/02782/deutsche schallplatten (japan) TKCC 70284
	recording completed in march 1978

symphony no 6 in d op 60
recorded on 6 july 1979 in the christuskirche

staatskapelle berlin	lp: eterna 827 540/deutsche schallplatten (japan) ET 5098
	cd: berlin classics 02782/92962/deutsche schallplatten (japan) TKCC 70285
	recording completed in february 1980

symphony no 7 in d minor op 70
recorded between 22-26 february 1981in the christuskirche

staatskapelle berlin	lp: eterna 827 541/deutsche schallplatten (japan) ET 5128
	cd: berlin classics 02782/92962/deutsche schallplatten (japan) TKCC 70286

symphony no 8 in g op 88
recorded on 26 september 1975 at a concert in the staatsoper

staatskapelle berlin	unpublished radio broadcast *german radio archives*

recorded between 11-15 july 1977 in the christuskirche

staatskapelle berlin	lp: eterna 827 194/deutsche schallplatten (japan) ET 5017
	cd: berlin classics 02782/93112/deutsche schallplatten (japan) TKCC 70286

dvorak/**symphony no 9 in e minor op 95 "from the new world"**
recorded on 29-31 march 1978 in the christuskirche
staatskapelle berlin   lp: deutsche schallplatten (japan) ET 5039
                                       cd: berlin classics 02782/13392/21552/
                                       deutsche schallplatten (japan) TKCC 70287

amid nature, overture op 91
recorded on 20 february 1981 in the christuskirche
staatskapelle berlin   lp: eterna 827 539/deutsche
                                       schallplatten (japan) ET 5129
                                       cd: deutsche schallplatten (japan) TKCC 70282

carnival overture op 92
recorded between 22-26 february 1981 in the christuskirche
staatsapelle berlin   lp: eterna 827 541/deutsche
                                       schallplatten (japan) ET 5128
                                       cd: deutsche schallplatten (japan) TKCC 70287

husitska overture op 67
recorded on 2 july 1979 in the christuskirche
staatskapelle berlin   lp: eterna 827 292/deutsche
                                       schallplatten (japan) ET 5087
                                       cd: berlin classics 13392/21352/deutsche
                                       schallplatten (japan) TKCC 70281

my home, overture op 62
recorded on 28 march 1978 in the christuskirche
staatskapelle berlin   lp: eterna 827 195/deutsche
                                       schallplatten (japan) ET 5050
                                       cd: berlin classics 93112/deutsche
                                       schallplatten (japan) TKCC 70284

othello overture op 93
recorded on 4 september 1979 in the christuskirche
staatskapelle berlin   lp: eterna 827 540/deutsche
                                       schallplatten (japan) ET 5098/
                                       cd: deutsche schallplatten (japan) TKCC 70285

HANNS EISLER (1898-1962)
kleine sinfonie (1932)
recorded on 11 october 1964 at a concert in the staatsoper
staatskapelle berlin   unpublished radio broadcast
     german radio archives
recorded on 14 february 1975 at a concert in the staatsoper
staatskapelle berlin   unpublished radio broadcast
     german radio archives
recorded on 1 october 1982 at a concert in the staatsoper
staatskapelle berlin   unpublished radio broadcast
     german radio archives
ernste gesänge für bariton und streichorchester
recorded on 6 september 1963 at a concert in the schauspielhaus
staatskapelle dresden   cd: berlin classics 90582
leib

FRIEDRICH VON FLOTOW (1812-1883)
ach so fromm/martha
recorded between 1-18 december 1975 in the christuskirche
staatskapelle berlin   lp: eterna 826 665
büchner
mädchen brav und treu/martha
recorded in march 1977 in the christuskirche
staatskapelle berlin   lp: eterna 826 944/deutsche
chor der deutschen   schallplatten (japan) ET 5029
staatsoper   cd: berlin classics 83682

CHRISTOPH WILLIBALD GLUCK (1714-1787)
der betrogene kadi
recorded in july 1974 in the bürgerbräu munich
bayerisches   lp: emi 1C065 28834
staatsorchester   cd: cpo CPO 999 5522
chor der bayerischen   *excerpts*
staatsoper   cd: emi 567 6372
rothenberger, donath,
gedda, hirte, berry

CHARLES GOUNOD (1818-1893)
me voici ! d'ou vient ta surprise ?/faust
recorded on 12 february 1972 in the lukaskirche
staatskapelle dresden   lp: eterna 826 334
schreier, adam   cd: berlin classics 20432
sung in german

EDVARD GRIEG (1843-1907)
holberg suite
recorded between 8-11 june 1976 in the christuskirche

staatskapelle berlin   lp: eterna 826 878/deutsche
schallplatten (japan) ET 5002
cd: berlin classics 93932/2100 129
recording completed in december 1976

two movements from the lyric suite
recorded between 8-11 june 1976 in the christuskirche

staatskapelle berlin   lp: eterna 826 878/deutsche
schallplatten (japan) ET 5002
cd: berlin classics 93932/2100 129
recording completed in december 1976

norwegian dances op 35
recorded between 8-11 june 1976 in the christuskirche

staatskapelle berlin   lp: eterna 826 878/deutsche
schallplatten (japan) ET 5002
cd: berlin classics 93932/2100 129
recording completed in december 1976

peer gynt, first suite from the incidental music
recorded on 29 august 1952 in the kulturraum bamberg

bamberger symphoniker   lp: deutsche grammophon LP 16055/
LPE 17037/89675
cd: 477 5482/477 5494
selection from the suite
45: deutsche grammophon EPL 30002

peer gynt, second suite from the incidental music
recorded on 20-21 february 1953 in the kulturraum bamberg

bamberger symphoniker   lp: deutsche grammophon LP 16055/
LPE 17037/89675
cd: 477 5482/477 5494
selection from the suite
45: deutsche grammophon EPL 30002

three pieces from the sigurd jorsalfar suite
recorded between 8-11 june 1976 in the christuskirche

staatskapelle berlin   lp: eterna 826 878/deutsche
schallplatten (japan) ET 5002
cd: berlin classics 93932/2100 129
recording completed in december 1976

GEORGE FRIDERIC HANDEL (1685-1759)
acis and galatea
recorded on 23 november 1980 at a concert in tokyo
orchestra and soloists   unpublished radio broadcast
of the kunitacji
college of music

JOHANN ADOLF HASSE (1699-1783)
la serva scaltra
recorded in september 1979 in the christuskirche
staatskapelle berlin   lp: eterna 827 508
eisenfeld, süss   cd: berlin classics 91142
sung in german

FRANZ JOSEF HAYDN (1732-1809)
symphony no 100 "military"
recorded between 25-27 november 1965 in the heilandskirche leipzig
gewandhaus-orchester   lp: eterna 820 441/825 441/deutsche
        grammophon 135 107

violin concerto in c
recorded on 25-26 november 1964 in the christuskirche
staatskapelle berlin   lp: eterna 820 560/825 560/philips
suske   grandioso 894 046ZKY

violin concerto in g
recorded on 27 november 1964 in the christuskirche
staatskapelle berlin   lp: eterna 820 560/825 560
suske

PAUL HINDEMITH (1895-1963)
symphonic metamorphoses on themes by weber
recorded between 28 february-3 march 1967 in the lukaskirche
staatskapelle dresden   lp: eterna 825 843
        cd: berlin classics 00882/02442/02612/
        25716/30412/93942

symphony in e flat
recorded between 3-7 april 1968 in the christuskirche
staaatskapelle berlin   lp: eterna 825 843
        cd: berlin classics 80012

ENGELBERT HUMPERDINCK (1854-1921)
hänsel und gretel
recorded between 9-22 november 1969 in the lukaskirche

staatskapelle dresden   lp: eterna 826 177-178/telefunken
dresdner kreuzchor   DX 635 074
springer, hoff,   cd: berlin classics 20072/0220 007/
krahmer, schröter,   teldec ZA 835 074
schreier, adam   *excerpts*
    lp: eterna 825 663/826 179
    cd: berlin classics 02442/92932
    recording completed in february 1970

JOSEF LANNER (1801-1843)
hofballtänze
recorded between 16-20 march 1970 in the lukaskirche

staatskapelle dresden   lp: eterna 845 081
    cd: berlin classics 02612/10602/91452

schönbrunner walzer
recorded between 16-20 march 1970 in the lukaskirche

staatskapelle dresden   lp: eterna 845 081
    cd: berlin classics 02612/10602/
    90752/91452

steyrische tänze
recorded between 16-20 march 1970 in the lukaskirche

staatskapelle dresden   lp: eterna 845 081
    cd: berlin classics 02612/10602/
    90752/91452

FRANZ LISZT (1811-1886)
mazeppa
recorded between 22-25 february 1956 in the herkulessaal munich

bamberger symphoniker   lp: deutsche grammophon LPE 17086
    cd: 477 5482/477 5494

orpheus
recorded between 22-25 february 1956 in the herkulessaal munich

bamberger symphoniker   lp: deutsche grammophon LPE 17086
    cd: 477 5482/477 5494

ALBERT LORTZING (1801-1851)
die opernprobe
recorded in july 1974 in the bürgerbräu munich

bayerisches	lp: emi 1C065 28835/1C065 30741
staatsorchester	cd: cpo 999 5572
chor der bayerischen	*excerpts*
staatsoper	cd: emi 567 6372
lövaas, litz, gedda,	
hirte, berry	

in wein ist wahrheit; o wie köstlich ist das reisen/undine
recorded on 12 february 1972 in the lukaskirche

staatskapelle dresden	lp: eterna 826 334
schreier, adam	cd: berlin classics 20432

vater mutter schwestern brüder!/undine
recorded between 1-18 december 1975 in the christuskirche

staatskapelle berlin	lp: eterna 826 665
büchner	

GUSTAV MAHLER (1860-1911)
symphony no 1 in d "titan"
recorded on 22-24 may 1962 in the lukaskirche

staatskapelle dresden	lp: eterna 820 365/825 365/deutsche grammophon 2548 123
	cd: berlin classics 00682/02612/ 30372

televised in january 1984 at a concert in tokyo

nhk symphony	laserdisc: toshiba TOLW 3596

symphony no 2 in c minor "resurrection"
recorded between 22 november-2 december 1983 in the christuskirche

staatskapelle berlin	lp: eterna 827 875-876
chor der deutschen	cd: berlin classics 90112
staatsoper	
hajossyova, priew	

symphony no 5 in c sharp minot
recorded on 24-25 september 1984 in the christuskirche

staatskapelle berlin	cd: berlin classics 93422
	recording completed in december 1984

mahler/**vier lieder aus des knaben wunderhorn**
recorded on 1-2 march 1982 in the christuskirche

staatskapelle berlin lp: eterna 827 756/deutsche
lorenz schallplatten (japan) ET 5170
cd: berlin classics 93972

SIEGFRIED MATTHUS (born 1934)
die liebesqualen des catull, musikalisches drama
recorded on 25 september 1987 at a concert in the schauspielhaus

staatskapelle berlin unpublished radio broadcast
rundfunkchor berlin *german radio archives*
eisenfeld, junghans

ERNST HERMANN MEYER (1905-1988)
symphony in b flat

staatskapelle berlin lp: eterna 885 002

violin concerto
recorded on 2-4 march 1963 in the christuskirche

staatskapelle berlin lp: eterna 820 122/825 122/
oistrakh 820 363/825 363/885 057
cd: berlin classics 18461

recorded on 5 march 1965 at a concert in the staatsoper

staatskapelle berlin unpublished radio broadcast
oistrakh *german radio archives*

WOLFGANG AMADEUS MOZART (1756-1791)
symphony no 25 in g minor k183
recorded on 1 june 1963 in the heilandskirche leipzig

gewandhaus-orchester lp: eterna 820 441/825 441
recording completed in december 1963

symphony no 28 in c k200
recorded between 2-7 january 1974 in the lukaskirche

staatskapelle dresden lp: eterna 826 681/deutsche
schallplatten (japan) ET 3040
cd: berlin classics 02612/94732
recording completed in october 1974

mozart/**symphony no 29 in a k201**
recorded between 6-9 september 1960 in the lukaskirche
staatskapelle dresden   lp: eterna 820 222/825 222/825 109/
                               826 681/philips 894 041ZKY
                               cd: berlin classics 00422/02612/
                               94732

symphony no 30 in d k202
recorded in october 1974 in the lukaskirche
staatskapelle dresden   lp: eterna 826 682
                               cd: berlin classics 02612/94732

symphony no 31 in d k297 "paris"
recorded in april-may 1968 in the lukaskirche
staatskapelle dresden   lp: eterna 826 682
                               cd: berlin classics 02612/94732/
                               2100 108/MRC 008

symphony no 32 in g k318
recorded between 2-7 january 1974 in the lukaskirche
staatskapelle dresden   lp: eterna 826 683/deutsche
                               schallplatten (japan) ET 3041
                               cd: berlin classics 02612/94732

symphony no 33 in b flat k319
recorded on 10-11 april 1961 in the lukaskirche
staatskapelle dresden   lp: eterna 820 250/825 250/825 060/
                               826 683/deutsche schallplatten
                               (japan) ET 3041
                               cd: berlin classics 00432/02612

symphony no 34 in c k338
recorded between 2-7 january 1974 in the lukaskirche
staatskapelle dresden   lp: eterna 826 683/deutsche
                               schallplatten (japan) ET 3041
                               cd: berlin classics 02612/93942/
                               94732

mozart/**symphony no 35 in d k385 "haffner"**
recorded on 28-29 april 1968 in the lukaskirche
staatskapelle dresden   lp: eterna 826 102/deutsche
                        schallplatten (japan) ET 3042
                        cd: berlin classics 02612/94752/
                        2100 107/MRC 007

televised at a concert in yokohama
staatskapelle berlin   laserdisc: pioneer (japan)

symphony no 36 in c k425 "linz"
recorded on 18-19 may 1969 in the lukaskirche
staatskapelle dresden   lp: eterna 826 102/deutsche
                        schallplatten (japan) ET 3042/
                        emi 1C047 50809
                        cd: berlin classics 02612/94752/
                        2100 107/MRC 007

recorded on 6-7 january 1979 in the nhk studios tokyo
nhk symphony   cd: denon C37 7051

symphony no 38 in d k504 "prague"
recorded on 19-20 march 1968 in the lukaskirche
staatskapelle dresden   lp: eterna 826 645/deutsche
                        schallplatten (japan) ET 3042/
                        emi 1C047 50809
                        cd: berlin classics 02612/94752/
                        2100 108/MRC 008

recorded on 6-7 january 1979 in the nhk studios tokyo
nhk symphony   cd: denon C37 7051

recorded on 3 october 1984 at a concert in the schauspielhaus
staatskapelle berlin   cd: weitblick (japan) SSS 03422

mozart/**symphony no 39 in e flat k543**
recorded on 21-22 november 1974 in the lukaskirche
staatskapelle dresden   lp: eterna 826 511/826 852
                                    cd: berlin classics 02612/94762

recorded on 25 october 1978 at a concert in tokyo
staatskapelle berlin   cd: tokyo fm TFMC 0001

recorded on 17 december 1982 at a concert in tokyo
nhk symphony   cd: king KICC 3012

televised in january 1984 at a concert in tokyo
nhk symphony   laserdisc: pioneer (japan)

symphony no 40 in g minor k550
recorded on 17-18 march 1975 in the lukaskirche
staatskapelle dresden   lp: eterna 826 511/826 852
                                    cd: berlin classics 02612/94762

recorded on 25 october 1978 at a concert in tokyo
staatskapelle berlin   cd: tokyo fm TFMC 0001

recorded on 17 december 1982 at a concert in tokyo
nhk symphony   cd: king KICC 3012

televised in january 1984 at a concert in tokyo
nhk symphony   laserdisc: pioneer (japan)

symphony no 41 in c k551 "jupiter"
recorded on 5-6 march 1973 in the lukaskirche
staatskapelle dresden   lp: eterna 826 465/deutsche
                                    schallplatten (japan) ET 3040
                                    cd: berlin classics 00422/02612/94762

recorded on 25 october 1978 at a concert in tokyo
staatskapelle berlin   cd: tokyo fm TFMC 001

recorded on 17 december 1982 at a concert in tokyo
nhk symphony   cd: king KICC 3012

televised in january 1984 at a concert in tokyo
nhk symphony   laserdisc: pioneer (japan)

mozart/**string quintet in e flat k614, symphonic adaptation by paul dessau**
recorded on 16 october 1965 at a concert in the staatsoper
staatskapelle berlin   unpublished radio broadcast
                                german radio archives

recorded in may 1971 in the funkhaus nalepastrasse
staatskapelle berlin   lp: eterna 885 020/deutsche
                                schallplatten (japan) ET 5134
                                cd: berlin classics 91822/94722

recorded on 14 february 1975 at a concert in the staatsoper
staatskapelle berlin   unpublished radio broadcast
                                german radio archives

sinfonia concertante k297b, for 4 wind instruments and orchestra
recorded on 17-18 april 1961 in the lukaskirche
staatskapelle dresden   lp: eterna 820 809/825 809/826 715/
tolksdorf, schütte,   720 156/725 021/telefunken
wappler, schaffrath   SMT 1325/deutsche schallplatten
                                (japan) ET 3062
                                cd: berlin classics 00972/31302

flute and harp concerto in c k299
recorded on 17-18 march 1975 in the lukaskirche
staatskapelle dresden   lp: eterna 826 715/deutsche
walter, zoff   schallplatten (japan) ET 3062
                                cd: berlin classics 01192/31652

sinfonia concertante k364, for violin, viola and orchestra
recorded on 16 october 1965 at a concert in the staatsoper
staatskapelle berlin   unpublished radio broadcast
morbitzer, lipka   *german radio archives*

violin concerto no 5 in a k219
recorded on 5 march 1965 at a concert in the staatsoper
staatskapelle berlin   unpublished radio broadcast
oistrakh   *german radio archives*

mozart/**piano concerto no 15 in b flat k450**
recorded between 19-21 august 1963 in the lukaskirche
staatskapelle dresden   lp: eterna 820 464/825 464/
schmidt   philips fontana grandioso 894 046ZKY

piano concerto no 21 in c k467
recorded between 19-21 august 1963 in the lukaskirche
staatskapelle dresden   lp: eterna 820 464/825 464/
schmidt   philips fontana grandioso 894 046ZKY

ein musikalischer spass k522
recorded in april 1961 in the lukaskirche
staatskapelle dresden   lp: eterna 820 250/825 060
                                        cd: berlin classics 00442/02612/
                                        30142/32302

march in d k249
recorded between 23-29 august 1988 in the christuskirche
staatskapelle berlin   cd: denon CO 3007/CO 85184

serenade no 2 in d k101
recorded on 5-6 march 1973 in the lukaskirche
staatskapelle dresden   lp: eterna 826 477
                                        cd: berlin classics 00442/02612/
                                        26115/philips 426 0602

serenade no 6 in d k239 "serenata notturna"
recorded between 9-11 november 1960 in the lukaskirche
staatskapelle dresden   lp: eterna 820 222/825 222/826 477/
                                        philips 894 041ZKY
                                        cd: berlin classics 00442/02612/
                                        philips 426 0602

serenade no 7 in d k250 "haffner"
recorded between 21-29 august 1988 in the christuskirche
staatskapelle berlin   cd: denon CO 3007/CO 85184
batzdorf

mozart/**sertenade no 8 in d k286**
recorded on 5-6 march 1973 in the lukaskirche

staatskapelle dresden	lp: eterna 826 477/philips 6747 378
	cd: berlin classics 00422/02612/
	26115/philips 426 0602

serenade no 13 in g k525 "eine kleine nachtmusik"
recorded between 9-22 november 1960 in the lukaskirche

staatskapelle dresden	lp: eterna 820 222/825 222/
	826 477/philips 6527 036
	cd: berlin classics 00422/02612/
	26115/philips 426 0602

a berenice – sol nascente, concert aria k70
recorded between 24-27 april 1970 in the lukaskirche

staatskapelle dresden	lp: eterna 825 729
geszty	cd: berlin classics 02442/92832

fra cento affanni, concert aria k88
recorded between 24-27 april 1970 in the lukaskirche

staatskapelle dresden	lp: eterna 825 729
geszty	cd: berlin classics 02442/92832

ma che vi fece o stelle, concert aria k368
recorded between 24-27 april 1970 in the lukaskirche

staatskapelle dresden	lp: eterna 825 729
geszty	cd: berlin classics 02442/92832

männer suchen stets zu naschen, arietta k433
recorded between 9-13 november 1969 in the lukaskirche

staatskapelle dresden	lp: eterna 825 662/deutsche
adam	schallplatten (japan) ET 3004/ET 5034

mentre ti lascio oh figlia, concert aria k513
recorded in april 1962 in the lukaskirche

staatskapelle dresden	lp: eterna 826 662/deutsche
adam	schallplatten (japan) ET 3004/ET 5034

mia speranza adorata, concert aria k416
recorded between 24-27 april 1970 in the lukaskirche

staatskapelle dresden	lp: eterna 825 729
geszty	cd: berlin classics 02442/92832

mozart/**no che non sei capace, concert aria k419**
recorded in july 1961 in the lukaskirche
staatskapelle dresden   lp: eterna 827 043
vulpius   cd: berlin classics 09432/93432
           recording completed in september 1961

recorded between 24-27 april 1970 in the lukaskirche
staatskapelle dresden   lp: eterna 825 729
geszty   cd: berlin classics 02442/92832

non curo l'affetto, concert aria k74b
recorded between 24-27 april 1970 in the lukaskirche
staatskapelle dresden   lp: eterna 825 729
geszty   cd: berlin classics 02442/92832

per questa bella mano, concert aria k612
recorded in april 1962 in the lukaskirche
staatskapelle dresden   lp: eterna 826 662
adam

sperai vicino il lido, concert aria k368
recorded between 24-27 april 1970 in the lukaskirche
staatskapelle dresden   lp: eterna 825 729
geszty   cd: berlin classics 02442/92832

voi avete un cor fedele, concert aria k217
recorded between 24-27 april 1970 in the lukaskirche
staatskapelle dresden   lp: eterna 825 729
geszty   cd: berlin classics 02442/92832

vorrei spiegarvi oh dio!, concert aria k418
recorded in july 1961 in the lukaskirche
staatskapelle dresden   lp: eterna 827 043
vulpius   cd: berlin classics 09432/93432
           recording completed in september 1961

la clemenza di tito, overture
recorded between 5-14 january 1976 in the christuskirche
staatskapelle berlin   lp: eterna 826 936/deutsche
           schallplatten (japan) ET 3068
           cd: berlin classics 30462/32132/
           83982

mozart/**se all' impero!/la clemenza di tito**
recorded between 27-29 august 1967 in the lukaskirche

staatskapelle dresden	lp: eterna 820 772/825 772/deutsche
schreier	schallplatten (japan) ET 3006/ET 5033
	cd: berlin classics 13332/83692/83982

del piu sublime soglio/la clemenza di tito
recorded between 13-17 april 1970 in the christuskirche

staatskapelle berlin	lp: eterna 826 001
schreier	cd: berlin classics 91392/91412

cosi fan tutte
recorded between 19-28 may 1969 in the studio brunnenstrasse berlin

staatskapelle berlin	lp: eterna 826 113-115/eurodisc
chor der deutschen	XK 80408
staatsoper	cd: berlin classics 32992/83982/94442
casapietra, burmeister,	*excerpts*
geszty, schreier,	lp: eterna 826 117
leib, adam	cd: berlin classics 32662/94722
	recording completed in september and november 1969

cosi fan tutte, scenes sung in german
recorded between 19-28 may 1969 in the studio brunnenstrasse berlin

staatskapelle berlin	lp: eterna 826 116/eurodisc KR 86800
casapietra, burmeister,	cd: berlin classics 20452/30462/32662
geszty, schreier,	*excerpts*
leib, adam	lp: eurodisc 302 203.420

cosi fan tutte, overture
recorded on 31 march 1970 in the funkhaus nalepastrasse berlin

staatskapelle berlin	unpublished radio broadcast
	german radio archives

recorded between 5-14 january 1976 in the christuskirche

staatskapelle berlin	lp: eterna 826 936/deutsche
	schallplatten (japan) ET 3068
	cd: berlin classics 30462/32132

tradito schernito!/cosi fan tutte
recorded between 27-29 august 1967 in the lukaskirche

staatskapelle dresden	lp: eterna 829 772/825 772/deutsche
schreier	schallplatten (japan) ET 3006/ET 5033
	cd: berlin classics 13332/83692/83982

mozart/**un aura amorosa/cosi fan tutte**
recorded between 27-29 august 1967 in the lukaskirche

staatskapelle dresden	lp: eterna 820 772/825 772/deutsche
schreier	schallpatten (japan) ET 3006/ET 5033
	cd: berlin classics 13332/83692/83982/
	91392/91412

rivolgete a lui lo sguardo/cosi fan tutte
recorded between 23-25 october 1966 in the lukaskirche

staatskapelle dresden	lp: eterna 820 739/825 739/
prey	emi 1C063 29087
	cd: berlin classics 13182/31492/
	32612/83982

donne mie le fate e tanti/cosi fan tutte
recorded between 23-25 october 1966 in the lukaskirche

staatskapelle dresden	lp: eterna 820 739/825 739/
prey	emi 1C063 29087
	cd: berlin classics 13182/31492/
	32612/83892

don giovanni, overture
recorded on 31 march 1970 in the funkhaus nalepastrasse berlin

staatskapelle berlin	cd: pilz acanta

recorded between 5-14 january 1976 in the christuskirche

staatskapelle berlin	lp: eterna 826 936/deutsche
	schallplatten (japan) ET 3068
	cd: berlin classics 30462/32132/83982

crudele! non mi dir/don giovanni
recorded in june 1961 in the lukaskirche

staatskapelle dresden	cd: berlin classics 93432
vulpius	*recording completed in september 1961*

il mio tesoro/don giovanni
recorded between 27-29 august 1967 in the lukaskirche

staatskapelle dresden	lp: eterna 820 772/825 772/deutsche
schreier	schallplatten (japan) ET 3006/ET 5033
	cd: berlin classics 13332/83692/83982

mozart/**dalla sua pace/don giovanni**
recorded between 27-29 august 1967 in the lukaskirche
staatskapelle dresden   lp: eterna 820 772/825 772/deutsche
schreier   schallplatten (japan) ET 3006/ET 5033
     cd: berlin classics 13332/83692/83982/
     91392/91412

madamina il catalogo e questa/don giovanni
recorded between 9-13 november 1969 in the lukaskirche
staatskapelle dresden   lp: eterna 825 662/deutsche
adam   schallplatten (japan) ET 3004/ET 5034

fin ch' han dal vino/don giovanni
recorded between 23-25 october 1966 in the lukaskirche
staatskapelle dresden   lp: eterna 820 739/825 739/
prey   emi 1C063 29087
     cd: berlin classics 13182/31492/
     32612/82982

recorded between 9-13 november 1969 in the lukaskirche
staatskapelle dresden   lp: eterna 825 662/deutsche
adam   schallplatten (japan) ET 3004/ET 5034

deh vieni alla finestra/don giovanni
recorded between 23-25 october 1966 in the lukaskirche
staatskapelle dresden   lp: eterna 820 739/825 739/
prey   emi 1C063 29087
     cd: berlin classics 13182/31492/
     32612/82982

recorded between 9-13 november 1969 in the lukaskirche
staatskapelle dresden   lp: eterna 825 662/deutsche
adam   schallplatten (japan) ET 3004/ET 5034

ah pieta signori miei!/don giovanni
recorded between 9-13 november 1969 in the lukaskirche
staatskapelle dresden   lp: eterna 825 662/deutsche
adam   schallplatten (japan) ET 3004/ET 5034

mozart/**meta di voi qua vadamo/don giovanni**
recorded between 23-25 october 1966 in the lukaskirche

staatskapelle dresden	lp eterna 820 739/825 738/
prey	emi 1C063 29087
	cd: berlin classics 13182/31492/
	32612/83982

recorded between 9-13 november 1969 in the lukaskirche

staatskapelle dresden	lp: eterna 825 662/deutsche
adam	schallplatten (japan) ET 3004/ET 5034

ho capito signore!/don giovanni
recorded between 23-25 october 1966 in the lukaskirche

staatskapelle dresden	lp: eterna 820 739/825 739/
prey	emi 1C063 29087
	cd: berlin classics 13182/31492/
	32612/83982

die entführung aus dem serail
recorded in october-november 1961 in the lukaskirche

staatskapelle dresden	lp: eterna 820 297-299/825 307-299/
chor der staatsoper	philips A02230-02231L/835 118-119AY/
dresden	SFL 14000-14001/700 194-195WGY/
vulpius, rönisch,	6720 005/turnabout TV 34320-34321
apreck, förster,	cd: berlin classics 32392/91162
van mill	*excerpts*
	lp: eterna 820 039/820 256/820 304/
	820 372/825 116/825 304/philips
	GL 5670/SGL 5670/G03098L/
	837 008GY
	cd: berlin classics 93432

die entführung aus dem serail, overture
recorded on 31 march 1970 in the funkhaus nalepastrasse berlin

staatskapelle berlin	unpublished radio broadcast
	german radio archives

recorded between 5-14 january 1976 in the christuskirche

staatskapelle berlin	lp: eterna 826 936/deutsche
	schallplatten (japan) ET 3068
	cd: berlin classics 30462/32132/83982

mozart/**vivat bacchus!**/die entführung aus dem serail
recorded on 12 february 1972 in the lukaskirche
staatskapelle dresden   lp: eterna 826 334
schreier, adam   cd: berlin classics 20432

hier soll ich dich denn sehen?/die entführung aus dem serail
recorded between 27-29 august 1967 in the lukaskirche
staatskapelle dresden   lp: eterna 820 772/825 772/deutsche
schreier   schallplatten (japan) ET 3006/ET 5033
                           cd: berlin classics 13332/83692/83982

wenn der freude tränen fliessen/die entführung aus dem serail
recorded between 27-29 august 1967 in the lukaskirche
staatskapelle dresden   lp: eterna 820 772/825 772/deutsche
schreier   schallplatten (japan) ET 3006/ET 5033
                           cd: berlin classics 13332/83692/83982

ich baue ganz/die entführung aus dem serail
recorded between 27-29 august 1967 in the lukaskirche
staatskapelle dresden   lp: eterna 820 772/825 772/deutsche
schreier   schallplatten (japan) ET 3006/ET 5033
                           cd: berlin classics 13332/83692/83982

konstanze dich wiederzusehen?/die entführung aus dem serail
recorded between 27-29 august 1967 in the lukaskirche
staatskapelle dresden   lp: eterna 820 772/825 772/deutsche
schreier   schallplatten (japan) ET 3006/ET 5033/
                           eurodisc 302 203.420
                           cd: berlin classics 13332/83692/83982/
                           91392/91412

la finta giardiniera, overture
recorded between 5-14 january 1976 in the christuskirche
staatskapelle berlin   lp: eterna 826 936/deutsche
                           schallplatten (japan) ET 3068
                           cd: berlin classics 30462/32132/83982

nella guerra d'amore/la finta semplice
recorded between 13-17 april 1970 in the christuskirche
staatskapelle berlin   lp: eterna 826 001
schreier   cd: berlin classics 91392/91412

mozart/**idomeneo, overture**
recorded between 5-14 january 1976 in the christuskirche
staatskapelle berlin   lp: eterna 826 936/deutsche
                              schallplatten (japan) ET 3068
                              cd: berlin classics 30462/32132/83982

non temer amato bene/idomeneo
recorded in july 1961 in the lukaskirche
staatskapelle dresden   lp: eterna 827 043
vulpius   cd: berlin classics 09432/93432
                              recording completed in september 1961

fuor del mar/idomeneo
recorded between 13-17 april 1970 in the christuskirche
staatskapelle berlin   lp: eterna 826 001
schreier   cd: berlin classics 91392/91412

e tollerare io posso/lucio silla
recorded between 13-17 april 1970 in the christuskirche
staatskapelle berlin   lp: eterna 826 001
schreier   cd: berlin classics 91392/91412

le nozze di figaro
recorded between 17-24 august 1964 in the lukaskirche
staatskapelle dresden   lp: eterna 820 498-500/825 498-500/
chor der staatsoper   columbia C 91379-91381/STC
dresden   91379-91381/angel SIC 6002/
güden, rothenberger,   emi 1C137 29192-29193/1C149
mathis, berry, prey   30159-30161/1C183 30159-30161
sung in german   cd: berlin classics 20962/emi 769 9292
                              excerpts
                              lp: eterna 820 506/825 506/825 124/
                              columbia C 80860/SMC 80860/
                              emi 1C063 28994
                              cd: berlin classics 90792

le nozze di figaro, overture
recorded between 5-14 january 1976 in the christuskirche
staatskapelle berlin   lp: eterna 826 936/deutsche
                              schallplatten (japan) ET 3068
                              cd: berlin classics 30462/32132/83982

recorded on 25 october 1978 at a concert in tokyo
staatskapelle berlin   cd: tokyo fm TFMC 0001

mozart/**se vuol ballare**/**le nozze di figaro**
recorded between 23-25 october 1966 in the lukaskirche

staatskapelle dresden   lp: eterna 820 739/825 739/
prey   emi 1C063 29087
     cd: berlin classics 13182/31492/
     32612/83982

recorded between 9-13 november 1969 in the lukaskirche

staatskapelle dresden   lp: eterna 825 662/deutsche
adam   schallplatten (japan) ET 3004/ET 5034

non piu andrai/**le nozze di figaro**
recorded between 23-25 october 1966 in the lukaskirche

staatskapelle dresden   lp: eterna 820 739/825 739/
prey   emi 1C063 29087
     cd: berlin classics 13182/31492/
     32612/83982

recorded between 9-13 november 1969 in the lukaskirche

staatskapelle dresden   lp: eterna 825 662/deutsche
adam   schallplatten (japan) ET 3004/ET 5034

aprite un po quel occhi/**le nozze di figaro**
recorded between 23-25 october 1966 in the lukaskirche

staatskapelle dresden   lp: eterna 820 739/825 739/
prey   emi 1C063 29087
     cd: berlin classics 13182/31492/
     32612/83982

recorded between 9-13 november 1969 in the lukaskirche

staatskapelle dresden   lp: eterna 825 662/deutsche
adam   schallplatten (japan) ET 3004/ET 5034

hai gia vinta la causa!/**le nozze di figaro**
recorded between 23-25 october 1966 in the lukaskirche

staatskapelle dresden   lp: eterna 820 739/825 739/
prey   emi 1C063 29087
     cd: berlin classics 13182/31492/
     32612/83982/emi 769 5072

recorded between 9-13 november 1969 in the lukaskirche

staatskapelle dresden   lp: eterna 825 662/deutsche
adam   schallplatten (japan) ET 3004/ET 5034

mozart/**der schauspieldirektor, overture**
recorded between 5-14 january 1976 in the christuskirche

staatskapelle berlin   lp: eterna 826 936/deutsche
schallplatten (japan) ET 3068
cd: berlin classics 30462/32132/83982

**wer hungrig bei der tafel sitzt; ihr mächtigen seht
ungerührt/zaide**
recorded between 9-13 november 1969 in the lukaskirche

staatskapelle dresden   lp: eterna 825 662/deutsche
adam   schallplatten (japan) ET 3004/ET 5034

die zauberflöte
recorded between 27 june-4 july 1970 in the lukaskirche

staatskapelle dresden   lp: eterna 826 173-175/eurodisc
rundfunkchor leipzig   XGR 80584/292 375/rca VL 32530
donath, geszty, hoff,   cd: rca/bmg 74321 322402
schreier, neukirch,   *excerpts*
leib, adam, vogel   lp: eterna 826 176/826 334/
eurodisc 302 203.420
cd: berlin classics 01612/20432

die zauberflöte, overture
recorded between 5-14 january 1976 in the christuskirche

staatskapelle berlin   lp: eterna 826 935/deutsche
schallplatten (japan) ET 3068
cd: berlin classics 30462/32132/83982

recorded on 13 june 1988 at a concert in tokyo

staatskapelle berlin   cd: altus (japan) ALT 024

dies bildnis ist bezaubernd schön/die zauberflöte
recorded between 27-29 august 1967 in the lukaskirche

staatskapelle dresden   lp: eterna 820 772/825 772/deutsche
schreier   schallplatten (japan) ET 3006/ET 5033/
eurodisc 302 203.420
cd: berlin classics 13332/83692/
83982/91392/91412

mozart/**wie stark ist nicht dein zauberton/die zauberflöte**
recorded between 27-29 august 1967 in the lukaskirche

staatskapelle dresden	lp: eterna 820 772/825 772/deutsche
schreier	schallplatten (japan) ET 3006/ET 5033/
	eurodisc 302 203.420
	cd: berlin classics 13332/83692/83982

der vogelfänger bin ich ja!/die zauberflöte
recorded between 23-25 october 1966 in the lukaskirche

staatskapelle dresden	lp: eterna 820 739/825 739/
prey	emi 1C063 29087
	cd: berlin classics 13182/31492/32612/
	83982/emi 769 5072

recorded between 9-13 november 1969 in the lukaskirche

| staatskapelle dresden | lp: eterna 825 662/deutsche |
| adam | schallplatten (japan) ET 3004/ET 5034 |

ein mädchen oder weibchen/die zauberflöte
recorded between 23-25 october 1966 in the lukaskirche

staatskapelle dresden	lp: eterna 820 739/825 739/
prey	emi 1C063 29087
	cd: berlin classics 13182/31492/
	32612/83982

recorded between 9-13 november 1969 in the lukaskirche

| staatskapelle dresden | lp: eterna 825 662/deutsche |
| adam | schallplatten (japan) ET 3004/ET 5034 |

papagena! papageno!/die zauberflöte
recorded between 23-25 october 1966 in the lukaskirche

staatskapelle dresden	lp: eterna 820 739/825 739/
prey	emi 1C063 29087
	cd: berlin classics 13182/31492/
	32612/83982

o isis und osiris/die zauberflöte
recorded in march 1978 in the christuskirche

staatskapelle berlin	lp: eterna 826 944/deutsche
chor der deutschen	schallplatten (japan) ET 5029
staatsoper	cd: berlin classics 83682

OTTO NICOLAI (1810-1849)
horch die lerche singt im hain/die lustigen weiber von windsor
recorded between 1-18 december 1975 in the christuskirche
staatskapelle berlin   lp: eterna 826 665
büchner

o süsser mond/die lustigen weiber von windsor
recorded in march 1977 in the christuskirche
staatskapelle berlin   lp: eterna 826 944/deutsche
chor der deutschen   schallplatten (japan) ET 5029
staatsoper   cd: berlin classics 83682
                            recording completed in february 1978

HANS PFITZNER (1869-1949)
palestrina
recorded in june 1986 (acts one and three) and on 19-20 june 1988 (act two)
at concerts in the schauspielhaus
staatskapelle berlin   cd: berlin classics 10012
chor der deutschen
staatsoper
dresdner kreuzchor
nossek, lang, schreier,
schmidt, lorenz,
wlaschiha, hübner,
ketelsen, trekel,
bindszus

**das käthchen von heilbronn, overture, melodrama and
act three prelude**
recorded on 21-22 september 1981 in the christuskirche
staatskapelle berlin   lp: eterna 827 683
                            cd: berlin classics 02442/90262
                            recording completed in february 1982

SERGEI PROKOFIEV (1891-1953)
piano concerto no 2
recorded on 14 february 1975 at a concert in the staatsoper
staatskapelle berlin   unpublished radio broadcast
mogilewski   *german radio archives*

piano concerto no 3
recorded on 1 october 1982 at a concert in the staatsoper
staatskapelle berlin   unpublished radio broadcast
prats   *german radio archives*

GIACOMO PUCCINI (1858-1924)
tosca
recorded on 30 october 1983 at a performance in the staatsoper
staatskapelle berlin   cd: premiere (usa) 1384
chor der deutschen
staatsoper
casapietra, wenkoff,
adam

MAX REGER (1873-1916)
eine ballettsuite op 130
recorded between 24-31 august 1972 in the defa studios babelsberg
staatskapelle berlin   lp: eterna 826 390/eurodisc XK 86535
                              cd: berlin classics 00402/02442/
                              32242/83992/91232

beethoven-variationen op 86
recorded on 24-25 august 1972 in the defa studios babelsberg
staatskapelle berlin   lp: eterna 826 307
                              cd: berlin classics 02442/32242/
                              83992/91232

konzert im alten stil op 123
recorded on 28-29 june 1972 in the christuskirche
staatskapelle berlin   lp: eterna 826 390/eurodisc XK 86535
                              cd: berlin classics 02442/32242/
                              83992/91232

reger/**variationen und fuge über ein thema von mozart** **op 132**
recorded on 16 october 1965 at a concert in the staatsoper
staatskapelle berlin   unpublished radio broadcast
german radio archives

recorded on 8 may 1987 at a concert in the schauspielhaus
staatskapelle berlin   unpublished radio broadcast
german radio archives

recorded on 25 september 1987 at a concert in the schauspielhaus
staatskapelle berlin   unpublished radio broadcast
german radio archives

GIOACCHINO ROSSINI (1792-1868)
il barbiere di siviglia
recorded between 7-14 february 1965 in the christuskirche
staatskapelle berlin   lp: eterna 820 572-574/825 572-574/
solistenvereinigung des   columbia C 91426-91428/SMC
berliner rundfunks   91426-91428/emi 1C137 29 12943
pütz, burmeister,   cd: berlin classics 90212/emi 769 3452
schreier, neukirch,   *excerpts*
prey, ollendorff,   lp: eterna 820 575/825 575/825 635
crass, kühne   cd: berlin classics 20412/94722
sung in german

ARNOLD SCHOENBERG (1874-1951)
fünf orchesterstücke op 16
recorded on 11 october 1964 at a concert in the staatsoper
staatskapelle berlin   unpublished radio broadcast
german radio archives

FRANZ SCHUBERT (1797-1828)
symphony no 1 in d d82
recorded between 8-12 july 1985 in the christuskirche
staatskapelle berlin   lp: eterna 725 046/denon
                              COCO 80571-80575
                              cd: denon C37 7905

symphony no 2 in b flat d125
recorded between 8-12 july 1985 in the christuskirche
staatskapelle berlin   lp: eterna 725 046/denon
                              COCO 80571-80575
                              cd: denon C37 7905

symphony no 3 in d d200
recorded between 23-26 june 1986 in the christuskirche
staatskapelle berlin   lp: eterna 725 150/denon
                              COCO 80571-80575
                              cd: denon CO 1253

symphony no 4 in c minor d417 "tragic"
recorded on 3-4 july 1985 in the christuskirche
staatskapelle berlin   lp: eterna 725 065/denon
                              COCO 80571-80575
                              cd: denon C37 7759

symphony no 5 in b flat d485
recorded between 1-5 july 1983 in the christuskirche
staatskapelle berlin   lp: eterna 725 008/denon
                              COCO 80571-80575
                              cd: denon C37 7156

symphony no 6 in c d589
recorded between 23-26 june 1986 in the christuskirche
staatskapelle berlin   lp: eterna 725 150/denon
                              COCO 80571-80575
                              cd: denon CO 1253

schubert/**symphony no 8 in b minor d759 "unfinished"**
recorded on 14 october 1978 at a concert in the staatsoper
staatskapelle berlin   unpublished radio broadcast
                              german radio archives

recorded between 1-5 july 1983 in the christuskirche
staatskapelle berlin   lp: eterna 725 008/denon
                              COCO 80571-80575
                              cd: denon C37 7156
                              also published on cd by union square music

televised in january 1984 at a concert in tokyo
nhk symphony   laserdisc: toshiba (japan)

symphony no 9 in c d944 "great"
recorded on 14 october 1978 at a concert in the staatsoper
staatskapelle berlin   unpublished radio broadcast
                              german radio archives

recorded between 20-24 september 1984 in the christuskirche
staatskapelle berlin   lp: eterna 725 090/denon
                              COCO 80571-80575
                              cd: denon C37 7371
                              also published on cd by union square music

recorded on 3 october 1984 at a concert in the schauspielhaus
staatskapelle berlin   unpublished radio broadcast
                              german radio archives

rosamunde, suite from the incidental music d797
comprising overture, ballet music no 1 in b minor, ballet music
no 2 in g and entr'acte no 3 in b flat
recorded between 10-12 july 1985 in the christuskirche
staatskapelle berlin   lp: eterna 725 065/denon
                              COCO 80571-80575
                              cd: denon C37 7759
                              also published on cd by union square music

schubert/**alfonso und estrella, opera in three acts d732**
recorded between 23 january-3 february 1978 in the christuskirche

staatskapelle berlin   lp: eterna 827 161-163/emi
rundfunkchor berlin   1C157 30816-30818/angel SCLX 3878
mathis, falewicz,   cd: berlin classics 21562
schreier, büchner,   *excerpts*
prey, adam,   lp: emi EX 29 04323
fischer-dieskau   cd: berlin classics 94722

2 marches caracteristiques d886, arranged for orchestra by wilckens
recorded between 27-29 september 1965 in the funkhaus nalepastrasse
staatskapelle berlin   cd: pilz acanta 44 20552

allegro in a minor "lebensstürme" d947, arranged for orchestra by wilckens
recorded between 27-29 september 1965 in the funkhaus nalepastrasse berlin
staatskapelle berlin   unpublished radio broadcast
                          german radio archives

MANFRED SCHUBERT (born 1937)
canzoni amorosi
recorded between 23-25 february 1974 in the funkhaus nalepastrasse berlin
staatskapelle berlin   lp: eterna 885 108
leib   cd: berlin classics 94722

recorded on 5 march 1987 at a concert in the schauspielhaus
staatskapelle berlin   unpublished radio broadcast
leib   *german radio archives*

ROBERT SCHUMANN (1810-1856)
symphony no 1 in b flat op 38 "spring"
recorded between 26 june-2 july 1986 in the christuskirche
staatskapelle berlin   lp: eterna 729 224-225
                          cd: denon CO 1516

recorded on 5 march 1987 at a concert in the schauspielhaus
staatskapelle berlin   unpublished radio broadcast
                          german radio archives

schumann/**symphony no 2 in c op 61**
recorded between 13-19 august 1987 in the christuskirche
staatskapelle berlin   lp: eterna 729 224-225
                              cd: denon CO 1967

symphony no 3 in e flat op 97 "rhenish"
recorded between 26 june-2 july 1986 in the christuskitche
staatskapelle berlin   lp: eterna 729 224-225
                              cd: denon CO 1516

symphony no 4 in d minor op 120
recorded between 13-19 august 1987 in the christuskirche
staatskapelle berlin   lp: eterna 729 224-225
                              cd: denon CO 1967

cello concerto in a minor op 129
recorded on 11 october 1964 at a concert in the staatsoper
staatskapelle berlin   unpublished radio broadcast
tortelier   *german radio archives*

BEDRICH SMETANA (1824-1884)
the bartered bride
recorded between 27 april-9 may 1962 in the lukaskirche
staatskapelle dresden   lp: eterna 820 326-328/825 326-328
chor der staatsoper   cd: berlin classics 20402/33012
dresden   *excerpts*
schlemm, burmeister,   lp: eterna 720 171/820 130/820 313/
apreck, neukirch, adam,   820 259/820 633/825 195/
leib, teschler   825 633/825 635
sung in german   cd: berlin classics 20402
                              recording completed in august 1962

komm mein söhnchen!/the bartered bride
recorded between 12-15 february 1972 in the lukaskirche
staatskapelle dresden   lp: eterna 826 334
schreier, adam   cd: berlin classics 20432
sung in german

JOHANN STRAUSS I (1804-1849)
radetzky march
recorded between 20-28 july 1979 in the lukaskirche
staatskapelle dresden   lp: eterna 845 205/deutsche
                             schallplatten (japan) ET 5096
                             cd: berlin classics 2153 121/94822

JOHANN STRAUSS II (1825-1899)
ägyptischer marsch
recorded in 1964 in the funkhaus nalepastrasse berlin
staatskapelle berlin   unpublished radio broadcast
                             german radio archives

an der schönen blauen donau, waltz
recorded on 4 december 1966 in the funkhaus nalepastrasse berlin
staatskapelle berlin   unpublished radio broadcast
                             german radio archives

recorded between 20-28 july 1979 in the lukaskirche
staatskapelle dresden   lp: eterna 845 205/deutsche
                             schallplatten (japan) ET 5096
                             cd: berlin classics 2153 121/94822

annen polka
recorded on 4 december 1966 in the funkhaus nalepastrasse berlin
staatskapelle berlin   unpublished radio broadcast
                             german radio archives

recorded between 20-28 july 1979 in the lukaskirche
staatskapelle dresden   lp: eterna 845 205/deutsche
                             schallplatten (japan) ET 5096
                             cd: berlin classics 2153 121/94822

elyen a magyar, polka
recorded between 20-28 july 1979 in the lukaskirche
staatskapelle dresden   lp: eterna 845 205/deutsche
                             schallplatten (japan) ET 5096
                             cd: berlin classics 2153 121/94822

die fledermaus, overture
recorded on 4 december 1966 in the funkhaus nalepastrasse berlin
staatskapelle berlin   unpublished radio broadcast
                             german radio archives

j.strauss II/**freikugeln, polka**
recorded between 20-28 july 1979 in the lukaskirche
staatskapelle dresden   lp: eterna 845 205/deutsche
                               schallplatten (japan) ET 5096
                               cd: berlin classics 2153 121/94822

künstlerleben, waltz
recorded between 20-28 july 1979 in the lukaskirche
staatskapelle dresden   lp: eterna 845 205/deutsche
                               schallplatten (japan) ET 5096
                               cd: berlin classics 2153 121/94822

unter donner und blitz, polka
recorded between 20-28 july 1979 in the lukaskirche
staatskapelle dresden   lp: eterna 845 205/deutsche
                               schallplatten (japan) ET 5096
                               cd: berlin classics 2153 121/94822

vergnügungszug, polka
recorded between 20-28 july 1979 in the lukaskirche
staatskapelle dresden   lp: eterna 845 205/deutsche
                               schallplatten (japan) ET 5096
                               cd: berlin classics 2153 121/94822

JOSEF STRAUSS (1827-1870)
auf ferienreisen, polka
recorded between 16-20 march 1970 in the lukaskirche
staatskapelle dresden   lp: eterna 845 081
                               cd: berlin classics 02612/90752/91452

dorfschwalben aus österreich, waltz
recorded between 20-28 july 1979 in the lukaskirche
staatskapelle dresden   lp: eterna 845 205/deutsche
                               schallplatten (japan) ET 5096
                               cd: berlin classics 2153 121/94822

feuerfest, polka
recorded between 16-20 march 1970 in the lukaskirche
staatskapelle dresden   lp: eterna 845 081
                               cd: berlin classics 02612/90752/91452

josef strauss/**frauenherz, polka**
recorded between 16-20 march 1970 in the lukaskirche
staatskapelle dresden   lp: eterna 845 081
                            cd: berlin classics 02612/91452

die libelle, polka
recorded between 16-20 march 1970 in the lukaskirche
staatskapelle dresden   lp: eterna 845 081
                            cd: berlin classics 02612/91452

mein lebenslauf ist lieb' und lust, waltz
recorded between 20-28 july 1979 in the lukaskirche
staatskapelle dresden   lp: eterna 845 205/deutsche
                            schallplatten (japan) ET 5098
                            cd: berlin classics 2153 121/94822

moulinet, polka
recorded between 16-20 march 1970 in the lukaskirche
staatskapelle dresden   lp: eterna 845 081
                            cd: berlin classics 02612/91452

plappermäulchen, polka
recorded between 16-20 march 1970 in the lukaskirche
staatskapelle dresden   lp: eterna 845 081
                            cd: berlin classics 02612/91452

JOHANN AND JOSEF STRAUSS
pizzicato polka
recorded between 16-20 march 1970 in the lukaskirche
staatskapelle dresden   lp: eterna 845 081
                            cd: berlin classics 02612/91452

RICHARD STRAUSS (1864-1949)
also sprach zarathustra
televised on 11 june 1964 at a strauss centenary concert in the schauspielhaus
staatskapelle dresden   unpublished video recording
                            ddr-fernsehen

strauss/**arabella, prelude to the third act**
recorded on 14 july 1970 in the funkhaus nalepastrasse

| staarskapelle berlin | lp: deutsche schallplatten (japan) ET 3005 |
| | cd: weitblick (japan) SSS 03422 |

ariadne auf naxos, prelude to the opera
recorded on 14 july 1970 in the funkhaus nalepastrasse

| staatskapelle berlin | lp: deutsche schallplatten (japan) ET 3005 |
| | cd: weitblick (japan) SSS 03422 |

der bürger als edelmann, suite from the incidental music
recorded in 1963 at a concert in dresden

| staatskapelle dresden | unpublished radio broadcast |
| | *german radio archives* |

kein andres das mir so im herzen loht/capriccio
recorded between 1-18 december 1975 in the christuskirche

| staatskapelle berlin | lp: eterna 826 665 |
| büchner | |

holla ihr streiter in apoll!/capriccio
recorded between 6-10 january 1969 in the lukaskirche

| staatskapelle dresden | lp: eterna 826 097/telefunken SAT 22513 |
| adam | cd: berlin classics 32562/91212/92152 |

seid ihr um mich ihr hirten alle?/daphne
recorded between 6-10 january 1969 in the lukaskirche

| staatskapelle dresden | lp: eterna 826 097/telefunken SAT 22513 |
| adam, schröter | cd: berlin classics 92152 |

don quixote
recorded on 3 october 1984 at a concert in the schauspielhaus

| staatskapelle berlin | unpublished radio broadcast |
| schumann, schröter | *german radio archives* |

strauss/**die frau ohne schatten**
recorded on 21 march 1971 at a performance in the staatsoper

staatskapelle berlin	unpublished radio broadcast
chor der deutschen	*german radio archives*
staatsoper	
tarres, dvorakova, kehl,	
vulpius, wenglor,	
prenzlow, ritzmann,	
neukirch, svorc, vogel	

sie aus dem hause!; sie haben es mir gesagt/die frau ohne schatten
recorded between 6-10 january 1969 in the lukaskirche

staatskapelle dresden	lp: eterna 826 097/827 407
chor der staatsoper	telefunken SAT 22513
dresden	cd: berlin classics 13222/92152
adam, schröter	

die frau ohne schatten, fantasie für grosses orchester
recorded on 15 july 1970 in the funkhaus nalepastrasse

staatskapelle berlin	lp: eterna 827 407/deutsche schallplatten (japan) ET 3005
	cd: berlin classics 02442/90262/94722

ein heldenleben
recorded on 5-6 february 1986 at a concert in tokyo

nhk symphony	cd: denon (japan)

horn concerto no 1
televised on 11 june 1964 at a strauss centenary concert in the schauspielhaus

staatskapelle dresden	unpublished video recording
buschner	*ddr-fernsehen*

metamorphosen
recorded between 8-11 june 1964 in the lukaskirche

staatskapelle dresden	lp: eterna 820 550/825 550
	cd: berlin classics 00882/02442/ 02612/25716/30232

televised on 11 june 1964 at a strauss centenary concert in the schauspielhaus

staatskapelle dresden	unpublished video recording
	ddr-fernsehen

58

strauss/**da lieg' ich/der rosenkavalier**
recorded between 6-10 january 1969 in the lukaskirche

staatskapelle dresden	lp: eterna 826 097/telefunken
chor der staatsoper	SAT 22513
dresden	cd: berlin classics 13222/92512
adam, schröter	

salome
recorded between 22-29 august 1963 in the lukaskirche

staatskapelle dresden	lp: eterna 820 375-376/825 375-376
goltz, eriksdotter,	cd: berlin classics 02442/32942/
melchert, hoppe,	91012
gutstein	*excerpts*
	lp: eterna 820 556/825 556

recorded on 4 october 1974 at a performance in the war memorial opera house san francisco

san francisco opera	cd: house of opera (usa)
orchestra	cd-rom: audio encyclopedia AE 201A
rysanek, varnay,	
hopf, nimsgern	

wie schön ist doch die musik/die schweigsame frau
recorded between 6-10 january 1969 in the lukaskirche

staatskapelle dresden	lp: eterna 826 097/telefunken
adam	SAT 22513
	cd: berlin classics 32562/91212/
	92152/93942

IGOR STRAVINSKY (1882-1971)
le sacre du printemps
recorded between 3-12 september 1962 in the lukaskirche

staatskapelle dresden	lp: eterna 720 174/725 174/
	820 984/825 984
	cd: berlin classics 00852/02612/
	25711/30352

l'oiseau de feu, suite from the ballet
recorded on 11 october 1964 at a concert in the staatsoper

staatskapelle berlin	unpublished radio broadcast
	german radio archives

FRANZ VON SUPPE (1819-1895)
banditenstreiche, overture
recorded in august 1969 in the lukaskirche
staatskapelle dresden   lp: eterna 845 053/philips 6580 113
                                    cd: berlin classics 02612/21532

dichter und bauer, overture
recorded in august 1969 in the lukaskirche
staatskapelle dresden   lp: eterna 845 053/philips 6580 113
                                    cd: berlin classics 02612/21532

flotte burschen, overture
recorded in august 1969 in the lukaskirche
staatskapelle dresden   lp: eterna 845 053/philips 6580 113
                                    cd: berlin classics 02612/21532

leichte kavallerie, overture
recorded in august 1969 in the lukaskirche
staatskapelle dresden   lp: eterna 845 053/philips 6580 113
                                    cd: berlin classics 02612/21532

ein morgen ein mittag ein abend in wien, overture
recorded in august 1969 in the lukaskirche
staatskapelle dresden   eterna unpublished

pique dame, overture
recorded in august 1969 in the lukaskirche
staatskapelle dresden   lp: eterna 845 053/philips 6580 113
                                    cd: berlin classics 02612/21532

die schöne galathea, overture
recorded in august 1969 in the lukaskirche
staatskapelle dresden   lp: eterna 845 053/philips 6580 113
                                    cd: berlin classics 02612/
                                    21532/90752

PIOTR TCHAIKOVSKY (1840-1893)
violin concerto in d op 35
recorded on 26 september 1975 at a concert in the staatsoper
staatskapelle berlin   unpublished radio broadcast
kulka   *german radio archives*

serenade for strings in c op 48
recorded between 5-8 november 1962 in the lukaskirche
staatskapelle dresden   lp: eterna 720 178/725 178/
                               820 961/825 961/deutsche
                               grammophon 135 109/2538 232/
                               2548 121/2705 004/2726 011
                               cd: berlin classics 02442/
                               02612/91942

GEORG PHILIPP TELEMANN (1681-1767)
der schulmeister, cantata
recorded on 1 april 1962 in the lukaskirche
staatskapelle dresden   lp: eterna 820 507/825 507
dresdner kreuzchor   cd: berlin classics 32002
adam

GIUSEPPE VERDI (1813-1901)
solenne in quest' ora/la forza del destino
recorded between 12-16 february 1972 in the lukaskirche
staatskapelle dresden   lp: eterna 826 334
schreier, adam   cd: berlin classics 20432
sung in german

GIOVANNI BATTISTA VIOTTI (1753-1824)
violin concerto no 22 in a minor
recorded on 22 march 1977 at a concert in the staatsoper
staatskapelle berlin   unpublished radio broadcast
kurosaki   *german radio archives*

ANTONIO VIVALDI (1678-1741)
concerto in d minor rv565
recorded on 12 june 1980 at a concert in the staatsoper
staatskapelle berlin   unpublished radio broadcast
                              german radio archives

ROBERT VOLKMANN (1815-1883)
serenade for strings no 2
recorded between 27-29 august 1967 in the lukaskirche

staarskapelle dresden   lp: eterna 820 961/825 961

cd: berlin classics 02442/02612/91942

RICHARD WAGNER (1813-1883)
der fliegende holländer
recorded on 11 august 1965 at a performance in the festspielhaus bayreuth

orchester und chor   unpublished radio broadcast
der bayreuther   *also unpublished video recording*
festspiele   *of rehearsal extracts*
silja, chookasian,
olvis, winkler,
stewart, greindl

die frist ist um/der fliegende holländer
recorded in november 1965 in the lukaskirche

staatskapelle dresden   lp: eterna 820 678/825 678
adam   cd: berlin classics 13222

recording completed in september 1966

willst jenes tags du dich nicht mehr entsinnen/der fliegende holländer
recorded between 12-16 june 1972 in the christuskirche

staatskapelle berlin   lp: eterna 826 538/cbs 77283
kollo   cd: berlin classics 13212/93792

recording completed in september 1972

recorded between 1-18 december 1975 in the christuskirche

staatskapelle berlin   lp: eterna 826 665
büchner

mit gewitter und sturm/der fliegende holländer
recorded between 12-16 june 1972 in the christuskirche

staatskapelle berlin   lp: eterna 826 538/cbs 77293
kollo   cd: berlin classics 13212/93792

recording completed in september 1972

summ und brumm/der fliegende holländer
recorded in march 1977 in the christuskirche

staatskapelle berlin   lp: eterna 826 944/deutsche
chor der deutschen   schallplatten (japan) ET 5029
springer   cd: berlin classics 83692

recording completed in february 1978

wagner/**götterdämmerung**
recorded on 17 october 1969 at a performance in the war memorial opera
house san francisco

san francisco opera	cd: house of opera (usa)
orchestra and chorus	cd-rom: audio encyclopedia AE 201A
shuard, martin, lilowa,	*recording may not be complete*
thomas, lagger, mazura	

brünnhilde heilige braut!/götterdämmerung
recorded between 12-16 june 1972 in the christuskirche

staatskapelle berlin	lp: eterna 826 539/cbs 77283
kollo	cd: berlin classics 93802/94722
	recording completed in september 1972

lohengrin, prelude
recorded on 15 april 1968 in the funkhaus nalepastrasse

staatskapelle berlin	unpublished radio broadcast
	german radio archives

recorded on 26-27 august 1972 in the christuskirche

staatskapelle berlin	lp: eterna 826 434
	cd: berlin classics 2100 147/13342

lohengrin, act three prelude
recorded on 15 april 1968 in the funkhaus nalepastrasse

staatskapelle berlin	unpublished radio broadcast
	german radio archives

recorded on 26-27 august 1972 in the christuskirche

staatskapelle berlin	lp: eterna 826 434
	cd: berlin classics 2100 147/13342

einsam in trüben tagen/lohengrin
recorded on 26-27 august 1972 in the christuskirche

staatskapelle berlin	lp: eterna 826 434
kuhse	cd: berlin classics 2100 147/13342

mein herr und gott!/lohengrin
recorded on 26-27 august 1972 in the christuskirche

staatskapelle berlin	lp: eterna 826 434
adam	cd: berlin classics 2100 147/13342

wagner/**nun sei bedankt mein lieber schwan/lohengrin**
recorded on 26-27 august 1972 in the christuskirche

staatskapelle berlin	lp: eterna 826 434
ritzmann	cd: berlin classics 2100 147/13342

erhebe dich genossin meiner schmach!/lohengrin
recorded on 26-27 august 1972 in the christuskirche

staatskapelle berlin	lp: eterna 826 434
dvorakova, stryczck	cd: berlin classics 2100 147/13342

höchstes vertrauen hast du mir schon zu danken/lohengrin
recorded between 12-16 june 1972 in the christuskirche

staatskapelle berlin	lp: eterna 826 538/cbs 77283
kollo	cd: berlin classics 13212/93792
	recording completed in september 1972

in fernem land/lohengrin
recorded between 12-16 june 1972 in the christuskirche

staatskapelle berlin	lp: eterna 826 538/cbs 77283
kollo	cd: berlin classics 13212/93792
	recording completed in september 1972

recorded on 26-27 august 1972 in the christuskirche

staatskapelle berlin	lp: eterna 826 434
ritzmann	cd: berlin classics 2100 147/13342

recorded between 1-18 december 1975 in the christuskirche

staatskapelle berlin	lp: eterna 826 665
büchner	

treulich geführt/lohengrin
recorded on 26-27 august 1972 in the christuskirche

staatskapelle berlin	lp: eterna 826 434
chor der deutschen	cd: berlin classics 2100 147/13342
staatsoper	

recorded in march 1977 in the christuskirche

staatskapelle berlin	lp: eterna 826 944/deutsche
chor der deutschen	schallplatten (japan) ET 5029
staatsoper	cd: berlin classics 83682
	recording completed in february 1978

wagner/**die meistersinger von nürnberg**

recorded on 1 october 1971 at a performance in the war memorial opera house san francisco

san francisco opera	cd: house of opera (usa)
orchestra and chorus	cd-rom: audio enterprises AE 201A
saunders, vanni, king,	
walker, adam, evans,	
flagello	

televised on 12 june 1980 at a performance in the staatsoper

staatskapelle berlin	dvd video: house of opera (usa)
chor der deutschen	DVDM 649
staatsoper	
casapietra, burmeister,	
wenkoff, schreier,	
adam, leib, olesch	

was duftet doch der flieder/die meistersinger von nürnberg

recorded in november 1965 in the lukaskirche

staatskapelle dresden	lp: eterna 820 678/825 678
adam	cd: berlin classics 00112/13222
	recording completed in september 1966

am stillen herd/die meistersinger von nürnberg

recorded between 12-16 june 1972 in the christuskirche

staatskapelle berlin	lp: eterna 826 538/cbs 77283
kollo	cd: berlin classics 13212/93792
	recording completed in september 1972

morgenlich leuchtend/die meistersinger von nürnberg

recorded between 12-16 june 1972 in the christuskirche

staatskapelle berlin	lp: eterna 826 538/cbs 77283
kollo	cd: berlin classics 13212/93792
	recording completed in september 1972

recorded between 1-18 december 1975 in the christuskirche

staatskapelle berlin	lp: eterna 826 665
büchner	cd: berlin classics 00112

wach auf!/die meistersinger von nürnberg

recorded in march 1977 in the christuskirche

staatskapelle berlin	lp: eterna 826 944/deutsche
chor der deutschen	schallplatten (japan) ET 5029
staatsoper	cd: berlin classics 83682
	recording completed in february 1978

wagner/**parsifal**
recorded on 20 september 1974 at a performance in the war memorial opera
house san francisco

san francisco opera	cd: house of opera (usa)
orchestra and chorus	cd-rom: audio enterprises AE 201A
randova, thomas,	
moll, stewart,	
booth, ginkel	

nach wilder schmerzensnacht/parsifal
recorded in november 1965 in the lukaskirche

staatskapelle dresden	lp: eterna 820 678/825 678
adam	cd: berlin classics 13222
	recording completed in september 1966

amfortas die wunde!/parsifal
recorded between 12-16 june 1972 in the christuskirche

staatskapelle berlin	lp: eterna 826 539/cbs 77283
kollo	cd: berlin classics 93802
	recording completed in september 1972

nur eine waffe taugt/parsifal
recorded between 12-16 june 1972 in the christuskirche

staatskapelle berlin	lp: eterna 826 539/cbs 77283
kollo	cd: berlin classics 93802
	recording completed in september 1972

das rheingold
recorded on 22 july 1967 at a performance in the festspielhaus bayreuth

orchester der bayreuther	unpublished radio broadcast
festspiele	*bayerischer rundfunk*
burmeister, silja, esser,	
windgassen, stewart,	
neidlinger, ridderbusch,	
böhme	

immer ist undank loges lohn/das rheingold
recorded between 1-18 december 1975 in the christuskirche

| staatskapelle berlin | lp: eterna 826 665 |
| büchner | cd: berlin classics 00112 |

wagner/**allmächtiger vater!**/rienzi
recorded between 12-16 june 1972 in the christuskirche

staatskapelle berlin	lp: eterna 826 538/cbs 77283
kollo	cd: berlin classics 13212/93792
	recording completed in september 1972

siegfried
recorded on 25 july 1967 at a performance in the festspielhaus bayreuth

orchester der bayreuther	unpublished radio broadcast
festspiele	*bayerischer rundfunk*
dvorakova, silja,	
höffgen, windgassen,	
wohlfahrt, greindl,	
neidlinger, böhme	

recorded on 2 october 1970 at a performance in the war memorial opera house san francisco

san francisco opera	cd: house of opera (usa)
orchestra	cd-rom: audio encyclopedia AE 201A
lindholm, thomas,	
stewart, ulfung	

dass der mein vater nicht ist/siegfried
recorded between 12-16 june 1972 in the christuskirche

staatskapelle berlin	lp: eterna 826 539/cbs 77283
kollo	cd: berlin classics 93802
	recording completed in september 1972

selige öde auf sonniger höh'/siegfried
recorded between 12-16 june 1972 in the christuskirche

staatskapelle berlin	lp: eterna 826 539/cbs 77283
kollo	cd: berlin classics 93802
	recording completed in september 1972

siegfried idyll
recorded on 15 april 1968 in the funkhaus nalepastrasse berlin

staatskapelle berlin	unpublished radio broadcast
	german radio archives

wagner/tannhäuser
recorded on 19 july 1964 at a performance in the festspielhaus bayreuth

orchester und chor	cd: melodram GM 10050/omega
der bayreuther	opera archive OOA 3933/opera
festspiele	lover TANN 196401
rysanek, ericson,	
windgassen, wächter,	
talvela	

*recorded on 12 october 1973 at a performance in the war memorial opera
house san francisco*

san francisco opera	cd: melodram GM 10082/house of opera
orchestra and chorus	(usa)/omega opera archive OOA 1426/
rysanek, napier,	opera lover TANN 197301
thomas, stewart, grant	cd-rom: audio encyclopedia AE 201A

televised in 1982 at a performance in the staatsoper

staatskapelle berlin	lp: platz PLCC 5001-5005
chor der deutschen	cd: gala GL 100 621/opera magic
staatsoper	24184
casapietra, dvorakova,	dvd video: premiere (usa) 5792
wenkoff, lorenz,	
hübner	

tannhäuser overture
recorded on 30 march 1970 in the funkhaus nalepastrasse berlin

staatskapelle berlin	cd: pilz acanta 44 20562

tannhäuser, venusberg music
recorded on 20 april 1968 in the funkhaus nalepastrasse berlin

staatskapelle berlin	cd: pilz acanta 44 20562

tannhäuser, act three prelude
recorded on 20 april 1968 in the funkhaus nalepastrasse berlin

staatskapelle berlin	cd: pilz acanta 44 20562

wagner/**inbrunst im herzen/tannhäuser**
recorded between 12-16 june 1972 in the christuskirche

staatskapelle berlin	lp: eterna 826 538/cbs 77283
kollo	cd: berlin classics 13212/93792
	recording completed in september 1972

recorded between 1-18 december 1975 in the christuskirche

staatskapelle berlin	lp: eterna 826 665
büchner	

freudig begrüssen wir die edle halle!; beglückt darf nun dich heimat ich schauen/tannhäuser
recorded in march 1977 in the christuskirche

staatskapelle berlin	lp: eterna 826 944/deutsche
chor der deutschen	schallpatten (japan) ET 5029
staatsoper	cd: berlin classics 83682
	recording completed in february 1978

tristan und isolde
recorded on 6 november 1970 at a performance in the war memorial opera house san francisco

san francisco opera	cd: house of opera (usa)
orchestra and chorus	cd-rom: audio encyclopedia AE 201A
nilsson, martin,	
windgassen, dooley,	
tozzi	

tristan und isolde, unspecified extract from act three
recorded on 13 march 1983 at a performance in the staatsoper

staatskapelle berlin	unpublished radio broadcast
wenkoff, neukirch,	*german radio archives*
svorc	

tatest du es wirklich?/tristan und isolde
recorded in november 1965 in the lukaskirche

staatskapelle dresden	lp: eterna 820 678/825 678
adam	cd: berlin classics 13222
	recording completed in september 1966

mild und leise/tristan und isolde
recorded in 1973 at a concert in stockholm

swedish radio orchestra	cd: opernwelt 2007
ligendza	

wagner/**die walküre**
recorded on 23 july 1967 at a performance in the festspielhaus bayreuth

orchester der bayreuther	unpublished radio broadcast
festspiele	*bayerischer rundfunk*
dvorakova, rysanek,	
mödl. king, stewart,	
greindl	

recorded on 20 october 1972 at a performance in the war memorial opera house san francisco

san francisco opera	cd: opera house (usa)/premiere
orchestra	(usa) 1863
nilsson, lindholm,	cd-rom: audio encyclopedia AE 201A
lilowa, thomas,	
stewart, grant	

ein schwert verhiess mir der vater/die walküre
recorded between 12-16 june 1972 in the christuskirche

staatskapelle berlin	lp: eterna 826 539/cbs 77283
kollo	cd: berlin classics 00112/93802
	recording completed in september 1972

winterstürme wichen dem wonnemond/die walküre
recorded between 12-16 june 1972 in the chrstuskirche

staatskapelle berlin	lp: eterna 826 539/cbs 77283
kollo	cd: berlin classics 93802
	recording completed in september 1972

leb wohl du kühnes herrliches kind/die walküre
recorded in november 1965 in the lukaskirche

staatskapelle dresden	lp: eterna 820 678/825 678
adam	cd: berlin classics 13222
	recording completed in september 1966

CARL MARIA VON WEBER (1786-1826)
symphony no 1 in c
recorded in april 1972 in the lukaskirche

staatskapelle dresden	lp: eterna 826 342/deutsche
	schallplatten (japan) ET 3003/
	eurodisc ZK 86472
	cd: berlin classics 02612/32472/
	90402

weber/**konzertstück for piano and orchestra**
recorded in august 1963 in the lukaskirche
staatskapelle dresden   eterna unpublished
schmidt

beherrscher der geister, overture
recorded in may 1974 in the christuskirche
staatskapelle berlin   lp: eterna 826 781/deutsche
schallplatten (japan)
ET 3025/ET 5030
cd: berlin classics 02442

die tale dampfen/euryanthe
recorded in march 1977 in the christuskirche
staatskapelle berlin   lp: eterna 826 944/deutsche
chor der deutschen   schallplatten (japan) ET 5029
staatsoper   cd: berlin classics 83682
recording completed in february 1978

der freischütz, overture
recorded on 25 september 1987 at a concert in the schauspielhaus
staatskapelle berlin   unpublished radio broadcast
german radio archives

was gleicht wohl auf erden/der freischütz
recorded in march 1977 in the christuskirche
staatskapelle berlin   lp: eterna 826 944/deutsche
chor der deutschen   schallplatten (japan) ET 5029
staatsoper   cd: berlin classics 83682
recording completed in february 1978

jubel, overture
recorded in may 1974 in the christuskirche
staatskapelle berlin   lp: eterna 826 781/deutsche
schallplatten (japan)
ET 3025/ET 5030
cd: berlin classics 02442

weber/**oberon, overture**
recorded in may 1974 in the christuskirche

| staatskapelle berlin | lp: eterna 826 781/deutsche schallplatten (japan) ET 3025/ET 5030 |
| | cd: berlin classics 02442 |

peter schmoll und seine nachbarn, overture
recorded in may 1974 in the christuskirche

| staatskapelle berlin | lp: eterna 826 781/deutsche schallplatten (japan) ET 3025/ET 5030 |
| | cd: berlin classics 02442 |

preziosa, overture
recorded in may 1974 in the christuskirche

| staatskapelle berlin | lp: eterna 826 781/deutsche schallplatten (japan) ET 3025/ET 5030 |
| | cd: berlin classics 02442 |

HUGO WOLF (1860-1903)
penthesilea, symphonic poem
recorded between 9-11 june 1980 in the christuskirche

| staatskapelle berlin | lp: eterna 827 683 |
| | cd: berlin classics 02442 |

recorded on 12 june 1980 at a concert in the staatsoper

| staatskapelle berlin | unpublished radio broadcast |
| | *german radio archives* |

MISCELLANEOUS
beliebte chöre aus italienischen und französischen opern
recorded between 7-9 june 1978 in the christuskirche

staatskapelle berlin	lp: eterna 827 120
chor der deutschen	cd: berlin classics 20212
staatsoper	*recording completed in july 1978*
kinderchor der dresdner	
philharmonie	

a copy of this recording was not available for precise verification purposes

Herbert Kegel 1920-1990

Born in Dresden, the city in which he also voluntarily ended his life
a year after the fall of the German Democratic Republic, Kegel
named the conductor Karl Böhm as being among his mentors.
As he was such an enthusiastic exponent of twentieth century music,
it was often overlooked, for example, what a convincing way he
had with the great Classical and Romantic choral works from Haydn's
Jahreszeiten through to Schoenberg's *Gurrelieder* and Mahler's Eighth
Symphony.

When planning their complete CD edition for the bi-centenary of
Mozart's death, Philips opted for a co-production with the Eterna
label when it came to the considerable body of lesser known
choral works, and these were what Kegel committed to disc with
his Dresden and Leipzig forces (although a few titles in the series
were actually recorded anonymously after Kegel's death). Another
important co-production, with the West German Capriccio label,
was Kegel's Beethoven symphony cycle, the first such undertaking
to be digitally recorded.

In the operatic field, highlights of Kegel's recorded work must
include a German-language version of Bizet's *Carmen*, Berg's
Wozzeck and Wagner's *Parsifal*.

RICHARD ADDINSELL (1904-1977)
warsaw concerto
recorded in 1969 in the lukaskirche

dresdner philharmonie	lp: eterna 825 646
stöckigt	cd: art 3671

TOMMASO ALBINONI (1671-1750)
adagio in g minot
recorded in 1986 in the lukaskirche

dresdner philharmonie	lp: eterna 725 152
	cd: eterna 729 152/capriccio 49314/
	laserlight 15688

JOHANN SEBASTIAN BACH (1685-1750)
air from the third orchestral suite
recorded on 18 october 1989 at a concert in the suntory hall tokyo

dresdner philharmonie	cd: altus (japan) ALT 056

musikalisches opfer, arranged by webern and dessau
recorded in may-june 1972 at concerts in the kongresshalle leipzig

rsol	cd: weitblick (japan) SSS 0602

BELA BARTOK (1881-1945)
concerto for orchestra
recorded on 29 september 1972 at a concert in the kongresshalle leipzig

rsol	cd: weitblick (japan) SSS 0252

divertimento for strings
recorded on 11-12 june 1961 in the kongresshalle leipzig

rsol	lp: eterna 820 277/825 277/
	deutsche grammophon 89 784
	cd: berlin classics 02332/31002

violin concerto no 2
recorded on 11-12 june 1961 in the kongresshalle leipzig

rsol	lp: eterna 820 278/825 278/deutsche
garay	grammophon 18 786/138 786
	cd: berlin classics 02332/31452

74

bartok/**viola concerto**
recorded between 14-16 march 1966 in the heilandskirche leipzig
rsol   lp: eterna 825 810
binder   cd: berlin classics 01432/01592/
                        02332/31252

cantata profana
recorded on 29 september 1972 at a concert in the kongresshalle leipzig
rsol   cd: weitblick (japan) SSS 0252
rundfunkchor leipzig
büchner, leib

LUDWIG VAN BEETHOVEN (1770-1827)
symphony no 1 in c op 21
recorded on 23-24 august 1983 in the lukaskirche
dresdner philharmonie   lp: eterna 725 020/729 020/
                         capriccio 95040
                         cd: capriccio 10001/49314
                         also published in sacd format by capriccio

symphony no 2 in d op 36
recorded on 25 september 1973 at a concert in the kongresshalle leipzig
rsol   cd: weitblick (japan) SSS 0272

recorded between 1-3 march 1982 in the lukaskirche
dresdner philharmonie   lp: eterna 725 020/729 020/
                         capriccio 95040
                         cd: capriccio 10001/49314
                         also published in sacd format by capriccio

symphony no 3 in e flat op 55 "eroica"
recorded on 2 september 1975 at a concert in the kongresshalle leipzig
rsol   cd: weitblick (japan) SSS 0512

recorded between 10-13 january 1983 in the lukaskirche
dresdner philharmonie   lp: eterna 725 020/729 021
                         capriccio 95040
                         cd: capriccio 10001/49314
                         also published in sacd format by capriccio

beethoven/**symphony no 4 in b flat op 60**
recorded between 1-4 february 1983 in the lukaskirche
dresdner philharmonie   lp: eterna 725 020/729 025/
                                    capriccio 95040
                                    cd: capriccio 10001/49314
                                    also published in sacd format by capriccio

symphony no 5 in c minor op 67
recorded between 14-18 june 1982 in the lukaskirche
dresdner philharmonie   lp: eterna 827 757/725 020/729 022/
                                    capriccio 95040
                                    cd: capriccio 10001/49314
                                    also published in sacd format by capriccio

recorded on 7 october 1986 at a concert in the schauspielhaus dresden
rsol   cd: weitblick (japan) SSS 0272

recorded on 18 october 1989 at a concert in the suntory hall tokyo
dresdner philharmonie   cd: altus (japan) ALT 056

symphony no 6 in f op 68 "pastoral"
recorded between 8-10 march 1983 in the lukaskirche
dresdner philharmonie   lp: eterna 720 020/729 022/
                                    capriccio 95040
                                    cd: capriccio 10001/49314
                                    also published in sacd format by capriccio

recorded on 18 october 1989 at a concert in the suntory hall tokyo
dresdner philharmonie   cd: altus (japan) ALT 055

symphony no 7 in a op 92
recorded between 16-20 september 1969 in the lukaskirche
staatskapelle dresden   cd: weitblick (japan) SSS 0582
                                    unpublished eterna lp recording

recorded between 20-22 october 1981 in the lukaskirche
dresdner philharmonie   lp: eterna 720 020/729 024/
                                    capriccio 95040
                                    cd: capriccio 10001/49314
                                    also published in sacd format by capriccio

beethoven/**symphony no 8 in f op 93**
recorded on 14 may 1974 at a concert in the kongresshalle leipzig
rsol   cd: weitblick (japan) SSS 0512

recorded in 1982-1983 in the lukaskirche
dresdner philharmonie   lp: eterna 720 020/729 022/
                                     capriccio 95040
                                     cd: capriccio 10001/49314
                                     also published in sacd format by capriccio

symphony no 9 in d minor op 125 "choral"
recorded on 4 august 1973 at a concert in berlin
rsob   unpublished radio broadcast
rundfunkchor berlin   *choral movement only*
casapietra, burmeister,   lp: eterna 826 548
büchner, adam

recorded between 20 may-7 june 1983 in the lukaskirche
dresdner philharmonie   lp: eterna 720 020/729 025/
rundfunkchor leipzig   capriccio 95040
rundfunkchor berlin   cd: capriccio 10001/49314
hargan, walther,   *also published in sacd format by capriccio*
büchner, kovacs   *recording completed in october 1983*

recorded on 31 july 1987 at a concert in the gewandhaus leipzig
rsol   cd: weitblick (japan) SSS 0662
rundfunkchor leipzig
gewandhauschor leipzig
rhuba-freiberger, lang,
schwartner, polster

piano concerto no 4 in g op 58
recorded on 6 june 1978 at a concert in the kongresshalle leipzig
rsol   cd: weitblick (japan) SSS 0682
richter-haaser

piano concerto no 5 in e flat op 73 "emperor"
recorded on 11 may 1971 at a concert in the kongresshalle leipzig
rsol   cd: weitblick (japan) SSS 0682
richter-haaser

beethoven/**triple concerto in c op 56**
recorded in 1986 in the lukaskirche
dresdner philharmonie   cd: capriccio 10150/49314
rösel, funke, timm

fantasy in c minor op 80, for piano, chorus and orchestra
recorded in 1985 in the lukaskirche
dresdner philharmonie   cd: capriccio 10150/49314
rundfunkchor leipzig
rösel

mass in c op 86
recorded between 25-28 november 1968 in the versöhnungskirche leipzig
gewandhaus-orchester   lp: eterna 826 119/telefunken
rundfunkchor leipzig   SAT 22512
kuhse, burmeister   cd: teldec ZK 841 286
schreier, adam

coriolan overture op 62
recorded between 14-18 june 1982 in the lukaskirche
dresdner philharmonie   lp: eterna 827 757/729 024
    cd: capriccio 10001

egmont overture op 84
recorded on 18 october 1989 at a concert in the suntory hall tokyo
dresdner philharmonie   cd: altus (japan) ALT 055

gott welch dunkel hier!/fidelio
recording date unspecified
rsol   cd: ponto PO 1033
gruber

ALBAN BERG (1885-1935)
violin concerto
recorded in july 1965 in the bethanienkirche leipzig
rsol   lp: eterna 820 538/825 538/
garay   deutsche grammophon 89 786

recorded on 26-27 march 1980 in the lukaskirche
dresdner philharmonie   lp: eterna 827 653
scherzer   cd: berlin classics 02332/02752/
    10122

berg/**wozzeck**
recorded on 9 april 1973 at a concert performance in the kongresshalle
leipzig

rsol	lp: eterna 826 656-657
rundfunkchor leipzig	cd: berlin classics 20682
dresdner kapellknaben	
schröter, adam,	
goldberg, hiestermann,	
wlaschiha	

wozzeck, fragments from the opera
recorded in july 1965 in the bethanienkirche leipzig

rsol	lp: eterna 820 538/825 538
kuhse	cd: berlin classics 02332/02752/
	90202

adagio from the lulu suite
recorded in july 1965 in the bethanienkirche leipzig

rsol	lp: eterna 820 538/825 538
	cd: berlin classics 02332/02752/
	90202

HECTOR BERLIOZ (1803-1869)
symphonie fantastique
recorded between 24-27 january 1984 in the lukaskirche

dresdner philharmonie	lp: eterna 827 931
	cd: berlin classics 02332/21482
	sacd: avex 25281
	also published on cd by deutsche
	schallplatten (japan)
	recording completed in may 1984

GEORGES BIZET (1838-1875)
carmen
recorded between 4-12 january 1960 in the kongresshalle leipzig

rsol	lp: eterna 820 172-173/deutsche
rundfunkchor leipzig	grammophon LPM 18 701-18 703/
und kinderchor	2701 008/2701 028
cervena, croonen,	cd: berlin classics 32952/91072
apreck, neukirch,	*excerpts*
lauhöfer, leib	lp: eterna 820 195/820 259/820 639/
sung in german	825 195/825 639/825 663/720 131
	cd: berlin classics 32482
	recording completed in march 1961

carmen, suite from the opera
recorded in 1987 in the lukaskirche

dresdner philharmonie	lp: eterna 725 173
	cd: berlin classics 94772

l'arlesienne, suites nos 1 and 2 from the incidental music
recorded in 1987 in the lukaskirche

dresdner philharmonie	lp: eterna 725 173
	cd: berlin classics 94772

jeux d'enfants
recorded in 1987 in the lukaskirche

dresdner philharmonie	lp: eterna 725 173
	cd: berlin classics 94772

BORIS BLACHER (1903-1975)
piano concerto no 2
recorded between 15-18 december 1980 in the lukaskirche

dresdner philharmonie	lp: eterna 827 521
herzog	cd: berlin classics 90152

konzertante musik
recorded on 15-16 april 1980 in the lukaskirche

dresdner philharmonie	lp: eterna 827 521
	cd: berlin classics 90152

80

blacher/**variationen über ein thema von paganini**
recorded on 15-16 april 1980 in the lukaskirche
dresdner philharmonie   lp: eterna 827 521
                             cd: berlin classics 90152

der grossinquisitor, oratorio after dostojevsky
recorded in may 1986 in the lukaskirche
dresdner philharmonie   lp: eterna 725 106
rundfunkchor leipzig   cd: berlin classics 93782
nimsgern

jüdische chronik
co-composition with dessau, henze, wagner-regeny and hartmann
see entry under miscellaneous on page 128

ALEXANDER BORODIN (1833-1887)
polovtsian dances/prince igor, arranged by rimsky-korsakov
recorded in 1970 in the lukaskirche
dresdner philharmonie   lp: eterna 825 646/826 027
rundfunkchor leipzig   cd: berlin classics 00862/01782/
sung in german   30052/32352

JOHANNES BRAHMS (1833-1897)
symphony no 1 in c minor op 68
recorded in 1961 at a concert in the kongresshalle
rsol   cd: ode classics (japan)

recorded on 27 march 1973 at a concert in the kongresshalle leipzig
rsol   cd: weitblick (japan) SSS 0222

symphony no 2 in d op 73
recorded on 23 november 1971 at a concert in the kongresshalle leipzig
rsol   cd: ode classics (japan) ODCL 1009/
                             pilz acanta

recorded on 22 november 1988 at a concert in the gewandhaus leipzig
rsol   cd: weitblick (japan) SSS 0622

brahms/symphony no 4 in e minor op 98
recorded between 2-5 september 1962 in the bethanienkirche
rsol   cd: ode classics (japan) ODCL 1010

recorded on 30 september 1983 at a concert in tokyo
nhk symphony   cd: king records (japan)

piano concerto no 2 in b flat op 83
recorded in 1979 in the lukaskirche
dresdner philharmonie   lp: eterna 827 423
schmidt   cd: denon DC 8086/COCO 70536

violin concerto in d op 77
recorded on 14 september 1961 at a concert in the kongresshalle leipzig
rsol   cd: ode classics (japan) ODCL 1011
garay

haydn variations op 56a
recorded on 14 september 1961 at a concert in the longresshalle leipzig
rsol   cd: ode classics (japan) ODCL 1011

ein deutsches requiem op 45
recorded on 27 march 1962 at a concert in the kongresshalle leipzig
rsol   unpublished radio broadcast
rundfunkchor leipzig   *german radio archives*
schlemm, lauhöfer

recorded in 1985 in the gewandhaus leipzig
rsol   lp: eterna 725 163/729 163
rundfunkchor leipzig   cd: capriccio 10095/49314
häggander, lorenz
*another performance of ein deutsches requiem conducted by kegel with the
nhk symphony orchestra and chorus on 28 september 1983 in tokyo
may have been published on cd in japan by king records*

schicksalslied op 54
recorded on 14 september 1961 at a concert in the kongresshalle leipzig
rsol   cd: ode classics (japan) ODCL 1011
rundfunkchor leipzig

REINER BREDEMEYER (1929-1995)
horn concerto
recorded in 1988 in the funkhaus nalepastrasse
staatskapelle berlin   cd: rca/bmg 74321 736582
weigle

BENJAMIN BRITTEN (1913-1976)
a war requiem
recorded in 1967 in the kongresshalle leipzig
rsol   lp: eterna 825 906-907
rundfunkchor leipzig   *excerpts*
und kinderchor   lp: eterna 826 985
kuhse, schreier, leib

televised in 1980 in the hofkirche dresden as a co-production between
ddr-fernsehen and bbc wales
bbc welsh orchestra   unpublished video recording
kammerorchester der   *ddr-fernsehen*
dresdener philharmonie
rundfunkchor leipzig
dresdner kapellknaben
gomez, tear, roberts

recorded in 1989 in the lukaskirche
dresdner philharmonie   cd: berlin classics 01012/02332/
rundfunkchor leipzig   deutsche schallplatten (japan)
dresdner kapellknaben
lövaas, roden, adam

young person's guide to the orchestra
recorded between 22-24 february 1971 in the lukaskirche
staatskapelle dresden   lp: eterna 826 305/eurodisc XBK 89518
r.ludwig   cd: denon COCO 84443/nova 970 032
narrated in german
les illuminations, song cycle
recorded on 9-10 november 1967 in the heilandskirche leipzig
rsol   lp: eterna 826 007
schreier   cd: berlin classics 90352
serenade for tenor, horn and orchestra
recorded on 9-10 november 1967 in the heilandskirche leipzig
rsol   lp: eterna 826 007
schreier, opitz   cd: berlin classics 90352

ANTON BRUCKNER (1824-1896)
symphony no 3 in d minor
recorded on 6 june 1978 at a concert in the kongresshalle leipzig
rsol   cd: ode classics (japan) ODCL 1012

recorded on 20 march 1986 at a concert in the gewandhaus leipzig
gewandhaus-orchester   cd: weitblick (japan)/lucky ball
                                          CDR 0020

symphony no 4 in e flat "romantic"
recorded on 11 november 1960 at a concert in the bethanienkirche leipzig
rsol   cd: weitblick (japan) SSS 0312

recorded in 1971 at a concert in the longresshalle leipzig
rsol   cd: ode classics (japan) ODCL 1014

symphony no 5 in b flat
recorded in 1977 at a concert in the kongresshalle leipzig
rsol   cd: ode classics (japan)

symphony no 6 in a
recorded in 1972 at a concert in the kongresshalle leipzig
rsol   cd: ode classics (japan)

symphony no 7 in e
recorded in 1961 at a concert in the kongresshalle leipzig
rsol   cd: ode classics (japan)

recorded in 1971 in the funkhaus leipzig
rsol   cd: ode classics (japan)

symphony no 8 in c minor
recorded in 1970 at a concert in the kongresshalle leipzig
rsol   cd: pilz acanta 44 20632/
                                          arioso ARI 110

recorded in 1975 at a concert in the kongresshalle leipzig
rsol   cd: ode classics (japan)

bruckner/**symphony no 9 in d minor**
recorded on 1 april 1969 at a concert in the kongresshalle leipzig
rsol   cd: ode classics (japan) ODCL 1021

recorded on 6 december 1975 at a concert in the kongresshalle leipzig
rsol   cd: ode classics (japan) ODCL 1022

te deum
recorded in 1979 in the funkhaus leipzig
rsol   cd: pilz acanta 44 20652
rundfunkchor leipzig
andor, burmeister,
büchner, vogel

MAX BUTTING (1888-1976)
symphony no 4
recorded on 1 november 1958 in the funkhaus leipzig
rsol   lp: eterna 820 487/885 146

symphony no 10
recorded between 1966-1968 in the kongresshalle leipzig
rsol   lp: eterna 825 868/885 169

stationen op 117
recorded in 1979 in the kongresshalle leipzig
rsol   lp: eterna 885 154

JOHANN CILENSEK (1913-1998)
symphony no 4
recorded on 1 november 1958 in the funkhaus leipzig
rsol   lp: eterna 820 487/885 146
                              cd: berlin classics 184502

horn concerto
recorded in 1985 in leipzig
rsol   lp: eterna 885 259
damm

LUIGI DALLAPICCOLA (1904-1975)
canti di prigonia, for chorus, two pianos, harps and
percussion
recorded in 1956 in the funkhaus leipzig
rsol   unpublished radio broadcast
rundfunkchor leipzig   *german radio archives*
reinelt, rögner

PAUL DESSAU (1894-1979)
die verurteilung des lukullus
recorded between 13-31 january 1964 in the bethanienkirche leipzig
rsol   lp: eterna 820 423-424/825 423-424/
rundfunkchor leipzig   820 557-558/885 129-130/
und kinderchor   telefunken SLT 43096-43097
krahmer, wenglor,   cd: berlin classics 10732/90602/
burmeister, prenzlow,   rca/bmg 74321 735042
melchert, barmeli,   *excerpts*
schall   lp: eterna 820 557/825 557
                                  recording completed in february, march and
                                  april 1964

deutsches miserere, oratorio
recorded on 20 september 1966 at a concert in the kongresshalle leipzig
rsol   unpublished radio broadcast
rundfunkchor leipzig   *excerpts*
müller   cd: rca/bmg 74321 735082

requiem für lumumba
recorded in 1964 in the kongresshalle leipzig
rsol   lp: eterna 885 010
rundfunkchor leipzig
geszty, bauer, schall,
naumann

hymnen 1959
recorded in 1966 in the kongresshalle leipzig
rsol   lp: eterna
rundfunkchor leipzig
krahmer, schall

dessau/**appell an die arbeiterklasse**
recorded in 1977 in the kongresshalle leipzig
rsol   lp: eterna 885 143
rundfunkchor leipzig
kinderchor der dresdner
philharmonie
burmeister, büchner

jüdische chronik
co-composition with blacher, henze, wagner-regeny and
hartmann
see entry under miscellaneous on page 128

orchestermusik no 2 "meer der stürme"
recorded in 1967 in the funkhaus leipzig
rsol   lp: eterna
                                        cd: berlin classics 02332/21822/
                                        184502

sonatina no 2 for piano and orchestra
recorded on 31 may 1976 at a concert in the kongresshalle leipzig
rsol   cd: pilz acanta 44 20772
stöckigt

KARL DIETRICH
dramatische szenen für flöte und orchester
recorded in 1970 in leipzig
rsol   lp: eterna 885 241
tast

PAUL-HEINZ DITTRICH (born 1930)
engführung, oratorio on texts by paul celan
recorded in 1988 in the lukaskirche
dresdner philharmonie   lp: eterna 885 291
vocal and instrumental   cd: berlin classics 2100 237/13052
ensembles
von osten

ANTONIN DVORAK (1841-1904)
symphony no 9 in e minor op 95 "from the new world"
recorded on 14 november 1967 at a concert in the kongreshalle leipzig
rsol   cd: weitblick (japan) SSS 0242

the devil and kate, overture
recorded in 1954 in the funkhaus leipzig
rsol   unpublished radio broadcast
                                       german radio archives

the noonday witch, symphonic poem
recorded in 1954 in the funkhaus leipzig
rsol   unpublished radio broadcast
                                       german radio archives

biblical songs for baritone and orchestra
recorded in 1988 in the lukaskirche
dresdner philharmonie   cd: berlin classics 91682
adam

requiem mass
recorded in 1988 at a concert in leipzig
rsol   unpublished radio broadcast
rundfunkchor leipzig   *german radio archives*
rundfunkchor berlin
casapietra, burmeister,
schreier, adam

stabat mater
recorded in 1952 at a concert in leipzig
rsol   unpublished radio broadcast
rundfunkchor leipzig   *german radio archives*
wenglor, fleischer,
lutze, öttel

GOTTFRIED VON EINEM (1918-1996)
das stundenlied, for chorus and orchestra
recorded in 1974 in the funkhaus leipzig
rsol   unpublished radio broadcast
rundfunkchor leipzig   *german radio archives*

HANNS EISLER (1898-1962)
fünf orchesterstücke (1938)
recorded on 14 june 1973 at a concert in the kongresshalle leipzig
rsol   cd: pilz acanta 44 20762

EDWARD ELGAR (1857-1934)
pomp and circumstance, march no 1
recorded in 1987 in the lukaskirche
dresdner philharmonie   lp: eterna 725 152/729 152
                               cd: capriccio 49314/
                               laserlight 15688

MANUEL DE FALLA (1876-1946)
ritual fire dance/el amor brujo
recorded in 1986 in the lukaskirche
dresdner philharmonie   lp: eterna 725 152/729 152
                               cd: capriccio 49314/
                               laserlight 15688

WOLFGANG FORTNER (1907-1987)
an die nachgeborenen, cantata
recorded in 1954 in the funkhaus leipzig
rsol   unpublished radio broadcast
rundfunkchor leipzig   *german radio archives*
lutze

FRITZ GEISSLER **(1921-1984)**
symphony no 3
recorded on 12 march 1968 in the funkhaus leipzig
rsol   lp: eterna 885 097/885 114
                                       cd: hastedt HT 5312

symphony no 5
recorded on 12 march 1968 in the funkhaus leipzig
rsol   lp: eterna 885 026
                                       cd: hastedt HT 5312
                                       excerpts
                                       cd: rca/bmg 74321 735162

symphony no 7
recorded in 1985 in leipzig
rsol   lp: eterna 885 234

piano concerto
recorded on 27 february 1977 in the kongresshalle leipzig
rsol   cd: hastedt HT 5312
arendt

italienische lustspielouvertüre, on themes of rossini
recorded on 21 november 1957 in the funkhaus leipzig
rsol   lp: eterna 820 530

GEORGE GERSHWIN **(1898-1937)**
rhapsody in blue, for piano and orchestra
recorded between 23-26 june 1975 in the kongresshalle leipzig
rsol   lp: eterna 740 035/840 046/
rundfunktanzorchester   845 046
stöckigt

an american in paris
recorded between 23-26 june 1975 in the kongresshalle leipzig
rsol   lp: eterna 740 035/840 046/
                                       845 046

MIKHAIL GLINKA **(1804-1857)**
russlan and lyudmila, overture
recorded in 1986 in the lukaskirche
dresdner philharmonie   lp: eterna 725 152/729 152
                                       cd: capriccio 49314/
                                       laserlight 15688

CHRISTOPH WILLIBALD GLUCK (1714-1787)
reigen seliger geister/orpheus und eurydike
recorded in 1986 in the lukaskirche

dresdner philharmonie	lp: eterna 725 152/729 152/
	825 646/826 930
	cd: capriccio 49314/
	laserlight 15688

FRIEDRICH GOLDMANN (born 1941)
symphony no 1
recorded in may-june 1973 in the kongresshalle leipzig

rsol	lp: eterna 885 166
	cd: berlin classics 02332/13022/
	90692/184502

CHARLES GOUNOD (1818-1893)
faust, scenes from the opera
recorded on 1 november 1967 in the kongresshalle leipzig

rsol	lp: eterna 826 197
rundfunkchor leipzig	cd: berlin classics 20342
casapietra, rotzsch,	*recording completed in april 1968*
schreier, schall, vogel	
sung in german	

EDVARD GRIEG (1843-1907)
herzwunden und letzter frühling/elegaic melodies
recorded in 1987 in the lukaskirche

dresdner philharmonie	lp: eterna 725 152/729 152
	cd: capriccio 49314/
	laserlight 15688

KARL AMADEUS HARTMANN (1905-1963)
symphony no 5
recorded on 18-19 april 1979 in leipzig
rsol   lp: eterna 827 432

symphony no 6
recorded between 12-14 february 1979 in leipzig
rsol   lp: eterna 827 432

symphony no 8
recorded in september 1971 in the funkhaus leipzig
rsol   lp: eterna 826 279
                                        cd: berlin classics 90482

violin concerto "concerto funebre"
recorded on 12-13 january 1971 in the bethanienkirche leipzig
rsol   lp: eterna 826 279
morbitzer

recorded between 12-15 january 1981 in the lukaskirche
dresdner philharmonie   lp: eterna 827 653
scherzer

jüdische chronik
co-composition with blacher, dessau, henze and wagner-regeny
see entry under miscellaneous on page 128

FRANZ JOSEF HAYDN (1732-1809)
die jahreszeiten
recorded between 20 january-5 february 1970 in the bethanienkirche leipzig
rsol   lp: eterna 826 370-372/eurodisc
rundfunkchor leipzig   XGK 85507/S 855046
stolte, schreier, adam   cd: rca/bmg 74321 491822/
                                        forlane UCD 16661-16662
                                        excerpts
                                        lp: eterna 826 339/826 985/
                                        eurodisc 200 158.250

symphony no 81 in g
recorded on 30 september 1986 at a concert in the gewandhaus leipzig
rsol   cd: weitblick (japan) SSS 0222

HANS WERNER HENZE (born 1926)
jüdische chronik
co-composition with blacher, dessau, hartmann and wagner-regeny
see entry under miscellaneous on page 128

PAUL HINDEMITH (1895-1963)
symphony in e flat
recorded on 18-19 january 1982 in the lukaskirche
dresdner philharmonie   lp: eterna 827 760
cd: berlin classics 90542/denon

sinfonia serena
recorded between 21-23 april 1981 in the lukaskirche
dresdner philharmonie   lp: eterna 827 760
cd: berlin classics 90542/denon
fourth movement
cd: rca/bmg 74321 735082

pittsburgh symphony
recorded on 13-14 august 1985 in the lukaskirche
dresdner philharmonie   lp: eterna 827 976
sacd: avex 25291
*also published on cd by deutsche
schallplatten (japan)*

mathis der maler symphony
recorded between 24-26 may 1980 in the lukaskirche
dresdner philharmonie   lp: eterna 827 542/deutsche
schallplatten (japan) ET 5115
cd: berlin classics 90542
*also published on cd by deutsche
schallplatten (japan)*

die harmonie der welt
recorded on 13-14 november 1984 in the lukaskirche
dresdner philharmonie   lp: eterna 827 976
cd: berlin classics 93912
sacd: avex 25291
*also published on cd by deutsche
schallplatten (japan)*

hindemith/**nobilissima visione**
recorded between 11-13 june 1980 in the lukaskirche
dresdner philharmonie   lp: eterna 827 542/deutsche
schallplatten (japan) ET 5115
cd: berlin classics 90542
sacd: avex 25291
also published on cd by deutsche
schallplatten (japan)

der schwanendreher, for viola and orchestra
recorded between 25-29 march 1968 in the heilandskirche leipzig
rsol   lp: eterna 826 134
lipka   cd: berlin classics 00962/30412

trauermusik for viola and orchestra
recorded on 16 march 1966 in the bethanienkirche leipzig
rsol   lp: eterna 825 810
binder   cd: berlin classics 02332/31252

bassoon concerto
recorded between 8-11 march 1982 in the lukaskirche
dresdner philharmonie   lp: eterna 827 797
königstedt

clarinet concerto
recorded between 8-11 march 1982 in the lukaskirche
dresdner philharmonie   lp: eterna 827 797
löchner

horn concerto
recorded between 12-14 may 1981 in the lukaskirche
dresdner philharmonie   lp: eterna 827 797
damm   cd: berlin classics

concerto for trumpet, bassoon and strings
recorded between 8-11 march 1982 in the lukaskirche
dresdner philharmonie   lp: eterna 827 797
güttler, königstedt   cd: berlin classics 90542

WOLFGANG HOHENSEE (born 1927)
hier bin ich mensch, five symphonic movements
recorded between 10-12 april 1969 in the lukaskirche
staatskapelle dresden   lp: eterna 825 920

LEOS JANACEK (1854-1928)
sinfonietta
recorded on 29 september 1972 at a concert in the kongreshalle leipzig
rsol   cd: weitblick (japan) SSS 0242

EMMERICH KALMAN (1882-1963)
gräfin maritza
recorded in 1954 in the funkhaus leipzig
rsol   lp: urania (usa) URLP 238
rundfunkchor leipzig   *excerpts published on lp in austria by*
richter, zorn, ritzmann,   *schallplattengilde gutenberg*
pallesche, westmayer

ARAM KHACHATURIAN (1903-1978)
waltz and galop from masquerade
recorded in 1971 in the lukaskirche
dresdner philharmonie   lp: eterna 825 646
                                 cd: art 3671/deutsche schallplatten
                                 (japan)

GUENTER KOCHAN (born 1930)
concerto for orchestra
recorded on 23-24 november 1962 in the funkhaus leipzig
rsol   lp: eterna 820 530/825 530/885 070

piano concerto
recorded between 27-29 march 1961 in the kongresshalle leipzig
rsol   lp: eterna 820 268/825 268/885 070
zechlin   cd: hastedt HT 5303

ZOLTAN KODALY (1882-1967)
psalmus hungaricus
recorded on 19 october 1953 in the funkhaus leipzig
rsol   unpublished radio broadcast
rundfunkchor leipzig   *german radio archives*
kozub

matra pictures, for unaccompanied chorus
recorded in 1957 in the funkhaus leipzig
rundfunkchor leipzig   45: eterna
sung in german   lp: eterna 730 001

RAINER KUNAD (1936-1995)
maitre pathelin, oder die hammelkomödie
recorded in 1974 in leipzig
rsol   lp: eterna 885 175
rundfunkchor leipzig
trekel-burkhardt,
hiestermann,
hölzke, polster

PAUL KURZBACH (1902-1997)
orchestervariationen; serenade; zigeunerlieder
recorded in 1977 in leipzig
rsol   lp: eterna 885 114

RUGGERO LEONCAVALLO (1858-1919)
intermezzo from I pagliacci
recorded in 1987 in the lukaskirche
dresdner philharmonie   lp: eterna 725 152/729 152
                                cd: capriccio 49314/
                                laserlight 15688

HORST LOHSE (born 1943)
symphony no 2
recorded in 1968 in leipzig
rsol   lp: eterna 885 124

GUSTAV MAHLER (1860-1911)
symphony no 1 "titan"
recorded on 9 may 1978 at a concert in the kongresshalle leipzig
rsol   cd: weitblick (japan) SSS 0302

recorded between 5-8 november 1979 in the lukaskirche
dresdner philharmonie   lp: eterna 827 438/deutsche
                                schallplatten (japan) ET 5089
                                cd: berlin classics 02332/02492/
                                90582
                                *also published on cd by deutsche
                                schallplatten (japan)*

recorded on 25 february 1981 at a concert in the kulturpalast
dresdner philharmonie   cd: weitblick (japan) SSS 0632

mahler/**symphony no 2 "resurrection"**
recorded on 15 april 1975 at a concert in the kongresshalle leipzig
rsol   cd: weitblick (japan) SSS 0302
rundfunkchor leipzig
breul, burmeister

symphony no 3
recorded on 25 march 1984 at a concert in the kulturpalast
dresdner philharmonie   cd: weitblick (japan) SSS 0282
philharmonischer chor
kinderchor der dresdner
philharmonie
majarowa

symphony no 4
recorded between 20-22 december 1976 in the paul-gerhardt-kirche leipzig
rsol   lp: eterna 827 183/deutsche
casapietra   schallplatten (japan) ET 5035
                                             cd: berlin classics 2100 148/
                                             13382/30182
                                             sacd: avex 25282
                                             recording completed in november 1977 and
                                             january 1978

symphony no 8 "symphony of a thousand"
recorded on 8 june 1981 at a concert in the kulturpalast
dresdner philharmonie   unpublished radio broadcast
rundfunkchor leipzig   *fragments from piano rehearsal on 6 june*
philharmonischer chor   *and orchestral rehearsal on 7 june*
kinderchor der dresdner   *published on a cd included with the*
philharmonie   *book ein dirigentenleben im 20. jahrhundert*
casapietra, termer,   *(see bibliography on page 8)*
riess, burmeister,
kollo, lorenz, polster

das klagende lied
recorded on 7 october 1985 at a concert in the gewandhaus leipzig
rsol   cd of the performance included
rundfunkchor leipzig   with the book *ein dirigentenleben im*
hajossyova, lang,   *20. jahrhundert* (see bibliography
korondi, kurth   on page 8)

FRANK MARTIN (1890-1975)
sechs monologe aus jedermann
recorded in 1987 in the lukaskirche
dresdner philharmonie   cd: berlin classics 91682
adam

SIEGFRIED MATTHUS (born 1934)
concerto for trumpet, timpani and orchestra
recorded in 1986 in the lukaskirche
dresdner philharmonie   lp: eterna 885 276
güttler, aigmüller   cd: berlin classics 90572

FELIX MENDELSSOHN-BARTHOLDY (1809-1847)
piano concerto no 1 in g minot op 25
recorded on 26-27 january 1972 in the versöhnungskirche leipzig
rsol   lp: eterna 826 330/deutsche
gheorgiu   grammophon 2535 416
    cd: berlin classics 90272

piano concerto no 2 in d minor op 40
recorded on 26-27 january 1972 in the versöhnungskirche leipzig
rsol   lp: eterna 826 330/deutsche
gheorgiu   grammophon 2535 416
    cd: berlin classics 90272/art 3626

concerto in a minor for piano and strings
recorded between 21-25 april 1975 in the bethanienkirche leipzig
rsol   lp: eterna 826 778
stöckigt   cd: berlin classics 01102/30892

capriccio brillant in b minor op 22 for piano and orchestra
recorded between 21-25 april 1975 in the bethanienkirche leipzig
rsol   lp: eterna 826 778
stöckigt

serenade and allegro in b minor op 43 for piano and orchestra
recorded between 21-25 april 1975 in the bethanienkirche leipzig
rsol   lp: eterna 826 778
stöckigt

auf flügeln des gesanges, choral arrangement
recording date unspecified
rundfunkchor leipzig   cd: deutsche schallplatten (japan)

ERNST HERMANN MEYER (1905-1988)
symphony for strings
recorded in february 1960 in leipzig

rsol	lp: eterna 820 171
	excerpt
	cd: rca/bmg 74321 735082

toccata appassionata
recorded between 11-14 february 1963 in the heilandskirche leipzig

rsol	lp: eterna 825 888

konzerante sinfonie, for piano and orchestra
recorded on 16-17 february 1962 in the funkhaus nalepastrasse berlin

rsol	lp: eterna 720 159/825 888/
zechlin	885 081
	third movement
	cd: rca/bmg 74321 735082

poem for viola and orchestra
recorded on 11-12 november 1964 in the heilandskirche leipzig

rsol	lp: eterna 820 530/825 810
binder	cd: berlin classics 02332/31252

WOLFGANG AMADEUS MOZART (1756-1791)
symphony no 22 in c k162
recorded on 22 october 1963 in the bethanienkirche leipzig

rsol	eterna unpublished

symphony no 23 in d k181
recorded on 28 october 1963 in the bethanienkirche leipzig

rsol	eterna unpublished

symphony no 28 in c k200
recorded on 25 october 1963 in the bethanienkirche leipzig

rsol	eterna unpublished

symphony no 29 in a k201
recorded on 17 may 1964 at a concert in the festsaal schloss altenburg

collegium musicum	unpublished radio broadcast
leipzig	*german radio archives*

mozart/**symphony no 40 in g minor k550**
recorded on 11 october 1966 at a concert in the kongresshalle leipzig
rsol   unpublished radio broadcast
                                        german radio archives
recorded in 1970 in the funkhaus leipzig
rsol   cd: pilz acanta 44 20642
recorded on 2 june 1987 at a concert in the gewandhaus leipzig
rsol   cd: weitblick (japan) SSS 0262

piano concerto no 18 in b flat k456
recorded between 26-30 september 1969 in the funkhaus leipzig
rsol   eterna unpublished
schmidt

piano concerto no 22 in e flat k482
recorded on 14 november 1967 at a concert in the kongresshalle leipzig
rsol   cd: weitblick (japan) SSS 0262
heidsieck   *also published by salzburg mozarteum*

bassoon concerto in b flat k191
recorded on 17 april 1964 in the funkhaus nalepastrasse berlin
rsob   unpublished radio broadcast
pischkitl   *german radio archives*

seven minuets k65a
recorded on 2 july 1964 in the bethanienkirche leipzig
rsol   eterna unpublished

ch' io mi scordi di te, concert aria with piano obbligato   k505
recorded on 20 december 1969 in the funkhaus leipzig
rsol   unpublished radio broadcast
breul, webersinke   *german radio archives*

zeffiretti lusinghieri/idomeneo
recorded on 16 may 1952 at a concert in the kongresshalle leipzig
rsol   unpublished radio broadcast
hofer   *german radio archives*
sung in german

mozart/**placido e il mar/idomeneo**
recorded on 16 may 1952 at a concert in the kongresshalle leipzig
rsol   unpublished radio broadcast
rundfunkchor leipzig   *german radio archives*
hofer
sung in german

qual nuovo terror!/idomeneo
recorded on 16 may 1952 at a concert in the kongresshalle leipzig
rsol   unpublished radio broadcast
rundfunkchor leipzig   *german radio archives*
sung in german

corriamo fuggiamo!/idomeneo
recorded on 16 may 1952 at a concert in the kongresshalle leipzig
rsol   unpublished radio broadcast
rundfunkchor leipzig   *german radio archives*
horand
sung in german

mass no 1 in g k49 "missa brevis"
recorded in june 1988 in the funkhaus leipzig
rsol   cd: philips 422 3562/422 5192/
rundfunkchor leipzig   426 8932/464 6482/
mathis, lang,   464 8602
heilmann, rootering

mass no 2 in d minor k65 "missa brevis"
recorded between 9-15 december 1987 in the funkhaus leipzig
rsol   cd: philips 422 2642/422 5192/
rundfunkchor leipzig   426 8932/464 6482/
donath, markert,   464 8602
heilmann, schmidt

mass no 3 in c k66 "dominicusmesse"
recorded in june 1988 in the funkhaus leipzig
rsol   cd: philips 422 3562/422 5192/
rundfunkchor leipzig   426 8932/464 6482/
mathis, lang,   464 8602
heilmann, rootering

mozart/**mass no 4 in c minor k139 "waisenhausmesse"**
recorded between 3-7 december 1973 in the versöhnungskirche leipzig

rsol	lp: eterna 826 579/philips
rundfunkchor leipzig	6598 688/6747 384
casapietra, burmeister,	cd: philips 422 5192/426 8932/
schreier, polster	464 6482/464 8602

missa brevis in g k140 "pastoralmesse"
recorded between 9-15 december 1987 in the funkhaus leipzig

rsol	cd: philips 422 2642/422 5192/
rundfunkchor leipzig	426 8932/464 6482/464 8602
donath, markert,	
heilmann, schmidt	

mass no 5 in c k167 "trinitasmesse"
recorded between 9-15 december 1987 in the funkhaus leipzig

rsol	cd: philips 422 2642/422 5192/
rundfunkchor leipzig	426 8932/464 6482/464 8602
donath, markert,	
heilmann, schmidt	

mass no 6 in f k192 "missa brevis"
recorded between 3-7 december 1973 in the versöhnungskirche leipzig

rsol	lp: eterna 826 580/philips
rundfunkchor leipzig	6500 867/6598 689
casapietra, burmeister,	cd: philips 422 5192/426 8932/
schreier, polster	464 6482/464 8602

mass no 7 in d k194 "missa brevis"
recorded between 3-7 december 1973 in the versöhnungskirche leipzig

rsol	lp: eterna 826 580/philips
rundfunkchor leipzig	6598 689
	cd: philips 422 5192/426 8932/
	464 6482/464 8692

mass in c k258 "piccolominimesse"
recorded between 22-25 november 1983 in the lukaskirche

dresdner philharmonie	lp: eterna 827 908/philips
rundfunkchor leipzig	412 2321
shirai, schiml,	cd: philips 412 2322/422 5192/
ude, polster	426 8932/464 6482/464 8602

mozart/**mass no 11 in c k259 "orgelsolomesse"**
recorded between 3-7 december 1973 in the versöhnungskirche leipzig

rsol	lp: eterna 825 580/philips
rundfunkchor leipzig	6500 867/6598 689/6747 384
casapietra, burmeister,	cd: philips 422 5192/426 8932/
schreier, polster	464 6482/464 8602

mass in c k262 "missa longa"
recorded between 22-25 november 1983 in the lukaskirche

dresdner philharmonie	lp: eterna 827 908/philips
rundfunkchor leipzig	412 2321
shirai, schiml,	cd: philips 412 2322/422 5192/
ude, polster	426 8932/464 6482/464 8602

mass no 13 in b flat k275 "missa brevis"
recorded in october 1985 in the funkhaus leipzig

rsol	cd: philips 422 5192/426 8932/
rundfunkchor leipzig	464 6482/464 8602
shirai, lang,	
baldin, polster	

mass no 15 in c k337 "missa solemnis"
recorded in october 1985 in the funkhaus leipzig

rsol	cd: philips 422 5192/426 8932/
rundfunkchor leipzig	464 6482/464 8602
shirai, lang,	
baldin, polster	

litaniae lauretanae in b flat k109
recorded between february 1979-february 1981 in leipzig

rsol	lp: eterna 827 648/philips 6725 015
rundfunkchor leipzig	cd: philips 422 5202/426 8942/
shirai, riess,	464 6482/464 8702
büchner, polster	

litaniae de venerabili altaris sacramento in b flat k125
recorded between february 1979-february 1981 in leipzig

rsol	lp: eterna 827 647/philips 6725 015
rundfunkchor leipzig	cd: philips 422 5202/426 8942/
shirai, riess,	464 6482/464 8702
büchner, polster	

mozart/**litaniae lauretanae in d k195**
recorded between 18 november-12 december 1974 in leipzig

rsol
rundfunkchor leipzig
frank-reinecke,
burmeister, büchner,
polster

lp: eterna 826 839/philips 6725 015
cd: philips 422 5202/426 8942/
464 6482/464 8702

litaniae de venerabili altaris sacramento in e flat k243
recorded between november 1974-december 1976 in leipzig

rsol
rundfunkchor leipzig
frank-reinecke,
burmeister, büchner,
polster

lp: eterna 826 840/philips 6725 015
cd: philips 422 5202/426 8942/
464 6482/464 8702

vesperae de dominica k321
recorded between february 1979-february 1981 in leipzig

rsol
rundfunkchor leipzig
shirai, riess,
büchner, polster

lp: eterna 827 648/philips 6725 015
cd: philips 422 5202/426 8942/
446 1972/464 6482/464 8702

alma dei creatoris k277, offertory
recorded between november 1974-december 1976 in leipzig

rsol
rundfunkchor leipzig
reinhardt-kiss,
burmeister, büchner

lp: eterna 826 839/philips 6725 015/
cd: philips 422 5202/426 8942/
464 6482/464 8702

ave verum corpus in d k618, motet
recorded in 1971 in the lukaskirche

dresdner philharmonie
rundfunkchor leipzig

lp: eterna 825 646/826 930
cd: art 3671
also published on cd by deutsche
schallplatten (japan)

benedictus sit deus k117, offertory
recorded in may 1990 in leipzig

rsol
rundfunkchor leipzig
schellenberger

cd: philips 422 5202/426 8942/
464 6482/464 8702

mozart/cibavit eos ex adipe frumenti k44
recorded in may 1990 in leipzig

rsol	cd: philips 422 5202/426 8942/
rundfunkchor leipzig	464 6482/464 8702
ribbe	

dixit et magnificat in c k193
recorded between february 1979-february 1981 in the funkhaus leipzig

rsol	lp: eterna 827 648/philips 6725 015
rundfunkchor leipzig	cd: philips 422 5202/426 8942/
shirai, büchner,	464 6482/464 8702
polster	

inter natos mulierum k72, offertory
recorded in may 1990 in leipzig

rsol	cd: philips 422 5202/426 8942/
rundfunkchor leipzig	464 6482/464 8702

kyrie in f k33
recorded in may 1990 in leipzig

rsol	cd: philips 422 5202/426 8942/
rundfunkchor leipzig	464 6482/464 8702

kyrie in d minor k90
recorded in may 1990 in leipzig

rsol	cd: philips 422 5202/426 8942/
rundfunkchor leipzig	464 6482/464 8702

kyrie in d k91
recorded in may 1990 in leipzig

rsol	cd: philips 422 5202/426 8942/
rundfunkchor leipzig	464 6482/464 8702

kyrie in e flat k322
recorded in may 1990 in leipzig

rsol	cd: philips 422 5202/426 8942/
rundfunkchor leipzig	464 6482/464 8702
schellenberger	

mozart/kyrie in c k323
recorded in may 1971 in leipzig

rsol   cd: philips 422 5202/426 8942/
rundfunkchor leipzig   464 6482/464 8702

kyrie in d minor k341
recorded in december 1976 in leipzig

rsol   lp: eterna 826 839/philips 6725 015/
rundfunkchor leipzig   cd: philips 422 5202/426 8942/
                              464 6482/464 8702

miserere mei deus k85
recorded in may 1990 in leipzig

rsol   cd: philips 422 5202/426 8942/
rundfunkchor leipzig   464 6482/464 8702

misericordias domini k222, offertory
recorded in november 1974 in leipzig

rsol   lp: eterna 826 840/philips 6725 015
rundfunkchor leipzig   cd: philips 422 5202/426 8942/
                              464 6482/464 8702

regina coeli k108
recorded in may 1990 in leipzig

rsol   cd: philips 422 5202/426 8942/
rundfunkchor leipzig   464 6482/464 8702
schellenberger

regina coeli k127
recorded between february 1979-february 1981 in the funkhaus leipzig

rsol   lp: eterna 827 647/philips 6725 015
rundfunkchor leipzig   cd: philips 422 5202/426 8942/
nawe   464 6482/464 8702

regina coeli k276
recorded between november 1974-december 1976 in leipzig

rsol   lp: philips 6725 015
rundfunkchor leipzig   cd: philips 422 5202/426 8942/
reinhardt-kiss,   464 6482/464 8702
burmeister, büchner,
polster

mozart/**sancta maria mater dei k273**
recorded between november 1974-december 1976 in leipzig

rsol	lp: philips 6725 015
rundfunkchor leipzig	cd: philips 422 5202/426 8942/
	464 6482/464 8702

scande coeli limina k34
recorded in may 1990 in leipzig

rsol	cd: philips 422 5202/426 8942/
rundfunkchor leipzig	464 6482/464 8702
schellenberger	

te deum laudamus k141
recorded between february 1979-february 1981 in the funkhaus leipzig

rsol	lp: eterna 827 647/philips 6725 015
rundfunkchor leipzig	cd: philips 422 5202/426 8942/
	464 6482/464 8702

veni sancte spiritus k47, offertory
recorded in may 1990 in leipzig

rsol	cd: philips 422 5202/426 8942/
rundfunkchor leipzig	464 6482/464 8702
schellenberger, lang,	
esching, pape	

venite populi k260, offertory
recorded in november 1974 in leipzig

rsol	lp: eterna 826 840/philips 6725 015
rundfunkchor leipzig	cd: philips 422 5202/426 8942/
	464 6482/464 8702

MODEST MUSSORGSKY (1839-1881)
pictures at an exhibition, arranged by ravel
recorded on 28 may 1959 in the funkhaus leipzig

rsol	lp: eterna 720 133/825 998
	cd: berlin classics 02332/30062/
	32352

recording completed in august 1959
recorded on 18 september 1980 at a concert in tokyo

nhk symphony	cd: king records (japan)

boris godunov, scenes from the opera, arranged by rimsky-korsakov
recorded on 1 may 1970 in the lukaskirche

staatskapelle dresden	lp: eterna 825 970/telefunken
rundfunkchor leipzig	SAT 22526/AS 641 290
kinderchor der dresdner	cd: berlin classics 20322/31622
philharmonie	
adam, kuhse, schreier,	
ritzmann, vogel	

sung in german

khovantschina, prelude to the opera arranged by rimsky-korsakov
recorded in 1987 in the lukaskirche

dresdner philharmonie	lp: eterna 725 152/729 152
	cd: capriccio 49314/
	laserlight 15688

LUIGI NONO (1924-1990)
come una ola de fuerza y luz, for soprano and piano
recorded between 7-9 july 1976 in the paul-gerhardt-kirche leipzig

rsol	lp: eterna 826 912/deutsche
reinhardt-kiss,	schallplatten (japan) ET 5041
la licata	cd: berlin classics 21412
	sacd: avex 25283
	also published on cd by deutsche
	schallplatten (japan)

epitaffio, three songs
recorded in 1963 in the funkhaus leipzig

rsol	unpublished radio broadcast
rundfunkchor leipzig	*german radio archives*
rist, hübenthal	

1977 recording of the work by eterna was conducted by horst neumann

CONNY ODD (born 1916)
in wald und auf der heide
recording date unspecified
rundfunkchor leipzig   lp: eterna 730 001
vulpius, hauchwitz

JACQUES OFFENBACH (1819-1880)
la belle helene, scenes from the operetta
recorded in 1969 in leipzig
rsol   lp: eterna 840 019
rundfunkchor leipzig   *excerpts*
roscher, morgan,   lp: eterna 840 001
klamm, jungwirth
sung in german

CARL ORFF (1895-1982)
die kluge
recorded in june 1976 in the paul-gerhardt-kirche leipzig
rsol   lp: eterna 827 155-156/
falewicz, büchner,   philips 6769 094
neukirch, lorenz,   cd: berlin classics 21042/94322
stryczek, süss   *some dialogue recorded later between*
                              april 1978-december 1980

der mond
recorded between february-may 1970 in the bethanienkirche leipzig
rsol   lp: eterna 826 332-333
rundfunkchor leipzig   cd: berlin classics 21042/94312
büchner, lunow,
süss, teschler

catulli carmina
recorded between 27-30 september 1971 in the versöhnungskirche leipzig
rsol   lp: eterna 826 374/philips 6500 815
rundfunkchor leipzig   cd: berlin classics 20472
mai, büchner

orff/**carmina burana**
recorded between 8-17 june 1960 in the funkhaus leipzig
rsol   lp: eterna 820 204/825 204/deutsche
rundfunkchor leipzig   gramophon 2535 275
kinderchor leipzig   cd: berlin classics 02332/32312
vulpius, rotzsch,
hübenthal

recorded between 16-18 october 1974 in the versöhnungskirche leipzig
rsol   lp: eterna 826 713/philips
rundfunkchor leipzig   9500 040/412 9331
jugendchor dresden   cd: berlin classics 20472/
casapietra, hiestermann,   philips 420 7132
stryczek   *recording completed in november-december 1974*

trionfo di afrodite
recorded between 11-13 june 1975 in leipzig
rsol   lp: eterna 826 841
rundfunkchor leipzig   cd: berlin classics 20472
nawe, kraemer,
büchner, hiestermann,
stryczek, süss

KRZYSZTOF PENDERECKI (born 1933)
threnos for the victims of hiroshima
recorded on 27 april 1978 in the bethanienkirche leipzig
rsol   lp: eterna 827 408
                             cd: berlin classics 02332/10122/83852

capriccio for violin and orchestra
recorded on 23-24 november 1977 in the lukaskirche
dresdner philharmonie   lp: eterna 827 408
wilkomirska   cd: berlin classics 83852

capriccio for oboe and strings
recorded on 28 may 1978 in the lukaskirche
dresdner philharmonie   lp: eterna 827 408
glätzner   cd: berlin classics 83852

als jakob erwachte
recorded on 11 november 1981 in the lukaskirche
dresdner philharmonie   lp: eterna 827 408
                             cd: berlin classics 83852

SERGEI PROKOFIEV (1891-1953)
betrothal in a monastery
recorded in 1971 in the funkhaus leipzig

rsol	lp: eterna 826 486
rundfunkchor leipzig	cd: berlin classics 20812
breul, croonen,	
burmeister, büchner,	
haseleu, polster,	
süss, kurth	

sung in german

the love of three oranges, suite from the opera
recorded between 13-15 november 1963 in the funkhaus leipzig

rsol	lp: eterna 820 381/825 381/
	eurodisc 201 991.250
	cd: berlin classics 01432/02332

peter and the wolf
recorded between 22-24 june 1971 in the lukaskirche

staatskapelle dresden	lp: eterna 826 305/eurodisc
r.ludwig	XBK 89518/201 991.250
narrated in german	cd: denon COCO 84443/
	nova 97 0032

GIACOMO PUCCINI (1858-1924)
gianni schicchi
recorded in 1971 in leipzig

rsol	lp: eterna 826 296
tomova-sintow, rupf	cd: berlin classics 20882

sung in german

MAURICE RAVEL (1875-1937)
l'enfant et les sortileges
recorded between 28 june-10 juky 1970 in the bethanienkirche leipzig
rsol   lp: eterna 826 341
rundfunkchor leipzig   cd: berlin classics 91182
springer, burmeister,   *recording completed in december 1970*
büchner, polster
sung in german

daphnis et chloe, second suite from the ballet
recorded in september 1965 at a concert in leipzig
rsol   cd: weitblick (japan)
rundfunkchor leipzig

piano concerto in g
recorded in march 1974 in the funkhaus leipzig
rsol   cd: weitblick (japan)
uhse

bolero
recorded in may 1985 in the funkhaus leipzig
rsol   cd: weitblick (japan)

EMIL VON REZNICEK (1860-1945)
donna diana, overture
recorded in 1971 in the lukaskirche
dresdner philharmonie   lp: eterna 825 646/827 505
                                               cd: art 3761

GIOACCHINO ROSSINI (1792-1868)
guillaume tell
recorded in july 1953 in the funkhaus leipzig
rsol   cd: walhall WLCD 0239
rundfunkchor leipzig
schubert-heuhaus,
hahnkamm, lutze,
horand, kaphan,
ramacher
sung in german

FRIEDRICH SCHENKER (born 1942)
symphony in memory of martin luther king
recorded in november 1974 in the bethanienkirche leipzig
rsol   lp: eterna 885 106

landschaften für grosses orchester
recorded in october 1975 in the funkhaus leipzig
rsol   lp: eterna 885 167
                              cd: berlin classics 02332/90692/
                              rca/bmg 74321 735122
                              recording completed in january 1976

CHRISTFRIED SCHMIDT (born 1932)
oboe concerto
recorded in 1985 in the lukaskirche
dresdner philharmonie   lp: eterna 725 152/
glätzner   729 152/885 255

EBERHARD SCHMIDT
thälmannlied/political song
recorded in 1955 in leipzig
rsol   78: eterna 110 058
rundfunkchor leipzig

FRANZ SCHMIDT (1874-1939)
notre dame, intermezzo
recorded in 1985 in the lukaskirche
dresdner philharmonie   lp: eterna 725 152/729 152
                              cd: capriccio 49314/
                              laserlight 15688/20006

ARNOLD SCHOENBERG (1874-1951)
verklärte nacht, version for string orchestra
recorded in 1958 in the funkhaus leipzig
gewandhaus-orchester   cd: berlin classics 02752

a survivor from warsaw
recorded on 17 april 1958 in the funkhaus leipzig
rsol   lp: eterna 820 201/825 201
rundfunkchor leipzig   cd: berlin classics 02752
lüdeke

schoenberg/**moses und aron**
recorded in 1976 in the paul-gerhardt-kirche leipzig
rsol lp: eterna 826 889-890/supraphon
rundfunkchor leipzig 1416211-1416212
dresdner kapellknaben cd: berlin classics 02332/11162
goldberg, haseleu
gurrelieder
recorded on 5 august 1986 in the lukaskirche
dresdner philharmonie lp: eterna 729 111-112
rsol cd: berlin classics 02332/90172
rundfunkchor leipzig
rundfunkchor berlin
prager männerchor
bundschuh, lang,
jung, appel, cold,
westphal

KURT SCHWAEN (born 1909)
lied der gewerkschaften/anthem of the trade unions
recorded in 1955 in leipzig
rsol 78: eterna 110 058
rundfunkchor leipzig 45: eterna 510 014

DIMITRI SHOSTAKOVICH (1906-1975)
symphony no 1 in f minor op 10
recorded between 13-17 november 1962 in the kongresshalle leipzig
rsol lp: eterna 720 188/820 675-676/
825 675-676
cd: berlin classics 01842/02332/
31702
symphony no 4 in c minor op 43
recorded in may 1969 at a concert in the kongresshalle leipzig
rsol cd: weitblick (japan)
symphony no 5 in d op 47
recorded on 14-15 may 1962 in the kongresshalle leipzig
rsol unpublished radio broadcast
german radio archives
recorded on 20 september 1980 at a concert in tokyo
nhk symphony cd: nhk (japan)
recorded in october 1986 at a concert in the schauspielhaus berlin
rsol cd: weitblick (japan)
symphony no 6 in b minor op 54
recorded in september 1973 at a concert in leipzig
rsol cd: weitblick (japan)

shostakovich/**symphony no 7 in c op 60 "leningrad"**
recorded on 16 may 1972 at a concert in the kongresshalle leipzig
rsol   cd: weitblick (japan) SSS 0282

symphony no 9 op 70
recorded in 1972 at a concert in the kongresshalle leipzig
rsol   unpublished radio broadcast
                                        german radio archives

recorded in may 1978 at a concert in the kongresshalle leipzig
rsol   cd: weitblick (japan)

symphony no 11 in g minor "the year 1905"
recorded in april 1958 at a concert in the kongresshalle leipzig
rsol   cd: weitblick (japan)

symphony no 14 op 135
recorded in march 1972 at a concert in the kongresshalle leipzig
rsol   cd: weitblick (japan)
petorsek, teschler
sung in german

symphony no 15 in a minor op 141
recorded in november 1972 at a concert in the kongresshalle leipzig
rsol   cd: weitblick (japan)

violin concerto no 2 in c sharp minor op 129
recorded on 10 october 1969 at a concert in the kulturpalast dresden
staatskapelle dresden   cd: weitblick (japan) SSS 0582
tretjakov

suite on verses of michelangelo op 145a
recording date unspecified
rsol   unpublished radio broadcast
nesterenko   *german radio archives*

the execution of stepan rasin op 119, cantata
recorded on 12 october 1967 in the haus auensee leipzig
rsol   lp: eterna 826 266/827 709/
rundfunkchor leipzig   philips 6585 012
vogel
sung in german

FRANZ SCHUBERT (1797-1828)
symphony no 8 in b minor d759 "unfinished"
recorded on 18 september 1980 at a concert in tokyo
nhk symphony   cd: king records (japan)

mass in g d167
recorded on 3 april 1979 at a concert in the kongresshalle leipzig
rsol   cd: pilz acanta 44 2065
rundfunkchor leipzig
stolte, weimann,
leib

recorded in september 1986 in the funkhaus leipzig
rsol   lp: eterna 827 101
rundfunkchor leipzig   cd: berlin classics 93412/2100 155
hajossyova, büchner,
polster

mass in e flat d950
recorded on 20 october 1954 at a concert in the kongresshalle leipzig
rsol   unpublished radio broadcast
rundfunkchor leipzig   *german radio archives*
wenglor, fleischer,
liebing, krämer

stabat mater d383
recorded in september 1986 in the funkhaus leipzig
rsol   lp: eterna 827 101
rundfunkchor leipzig   cd: berlin classics 93412/2100 155

MANFRED SCHUBERT (born 1937)
clarinet concerto
recorded in 1974 in the funkhaus leipzig
rsol   lp: eterna 885 075
michalik

ROBERT SCHUMANN (1810-1856)
symphony no 4 in d minor op 120
recorded on 14 october 1980 at a concert in the kongresshalle leipzig
dresdner philharmonie   cd: weitblick (japan) SSS 0622

recorded on 21 september 1983 at a concert in tokyo
nhk symphony   cd: king records (japan)

JEAN SIBELIUS (1865-1957)
symphony no 1 in e minor op 39
recorded on 26 april 1982 at a concert in the gewandhaus leipzig
rsol   cd: weitblick (japan)

symphony no 4 in a minor op 63
recorded on 1 december 1967 in the funkhaus leipzig
rsol   lp: eterna 826 135
          cd: berlin classics 01302/
          02332/32552

recorded on 4 march 1969 at a concert in the kongresshalle leipzig
rsol   cd: weitblick (japan)

valse triste op 44
recorded in 1986 in the lukaskirche
dresdner philharmonie   lp: eterna 725 152/729 152
          cd: capriccio 49314/
          laserlight 15688

CARL STAMITZ (1745-1801)
viola concerto in d
recorded between 25-29 march 1968 in the heilandskirche leipzig
rsol   lp: eterna 826 134
lipka

JOHANN STRAUSS II (1825-1899)
die fledermaus/concert version for radio
recorded in 1974 in the funkhaus leipzig
rsol   unpublished radio broadcast
rundfunkchor leipzig   *german radio archives*
voinea, trekel-burkhardt,
büchner, haseleu

an der schönen blauen donau, waltz
recording date unspecified
rsol   lp: urania (usa) URRS 7-21

recording date unspecified
rsol   lp: eterna 840 058/845 058

frühlingsstimmen, waltz
recording date unspecified
rsol   lp: urania (usa) URRS 7-21

g'schichten aus dem wienerwald, waltz
recording date unspecified
rsol   lp: eterna 840 058/845 058

künstlerleben, waltz
recording date unspecified
rsol   lp: eterna 840 058/845 058

JOSEF STRAUSS (1827-1870)
dorfschwalben aus österreich, waltz
recordimg date unspecified
rsol   lp: eterna 840 058/845 058

RICHARD STRAUSS (1864-1949)
ariadne auf naxos
recorded in 1954 in the funkhaus leipzig
rsol   cd: walhall WLCD 0231
friedland, ziese,   *according to jutta vulpius this radio*
vulpius, schüffler,   *performance was actually conducted*
wocke, lauhöfer,   *by paul schmitz*
schelske

richard strauss/**don quixote**
recorded in 1963 in the funkhaus leipzig
rsol   unpublished radio broadcast
tortelier, lipka   *german radio archives*

tod und verklärung
recorded in 1968 in the funkhaus leipzig
rsol   unpublished radio broadcast
                                       german radio archives

vier letzte lieder
recorded in 1972 in the funkhaus nalepastrasse berlin
rsob   unpublished radio broadcast
casapietra   *german radio archives*

IGOR STRAVINSKY (1882-1971)
capriccio for piano and orchestra
recorded on 26-27 january 1978 in the lukaskirche
dresdner philharmonie   lp: eterna 827 296/deutsche
rösel   schallplatten (japan) ET 5072
                            cd: berlin classics 02332/20442/
                            32112
                            also published on cd by deutsche
                            schallplatten (japan)

le chant du rossignol
recorded between 13-15 december 1983 in the lukaskirche
dresdner philharmonie   lp: eterna 827 614
                            cd: berlin classics 02332/20442
                            sacd: avex 25293

circus polka
recorded on 26-27 january 1978 in the lukaskirche
dresdner philharmonie   lp: eterna 827 296/deutsche
                            schallplatten (japan) ET 5072
                            cd: berlin classics 32112/
                            capriccio 49314

stravinsky/**dumbarton oaks, concerto**
recorded on 24 december 1970 in the funkhaus leipzig
rsol lp: eterna 826 542/deutsche
schallplatten (japan) ET 3050
cd: berlin classics 10922/31222
also published on cd by deutsche
schallplatten (japan)

jeu de cartes
recorded on 1 october 1973 in the funkhaus leipzig
rsol lp: eterna 826 542/deutsche
schallplatten (japan) ET 3050
cd: berlin classics 30352
also published on cd by deutsche
schallplatten (japan)

l'oiseau de feu, 1919 suite from the ballet
recorded on 1 april 1969 at a concert in the kongresshalle leipzig
rsol cd: weitblick (japan) SSS 0232

pulcinella suite
recorded between 23-25 june 1981 in the lukaskirche
dresdner philharmonie lp: eterna 827 614
cd: berlin classics 02332/20442/
32112
sacd: avex 25293

le sacre du printemps
recorded on 19 april 1977 at a concert in the kongresshalle leipzig
rsol cd: weitblick (japan) SSS 0232

suites nos 1 and 2 for small orchestra
recorded on 3 may 1971 (suite no 2) and 4 november 1971 (suite no 1)
in the bethanienkirche leipzig
rsol lp: eterna 826 542/deutsche
schallplatten (japan) ET 3050
cd: berlin classics 01012/31222
also published on cd by deutsche
schallplatten (japan)

scenes de ballet
recorded on 30 september 1986 at a concert in the gewandhaus leipzig
rsol cd: weitblick (japan) SSS 0232

120

MIKIS THEODORAKIS (born 1925)
symphony no 7 "spring symphony"
recorded in 1987 at a concert in the kulturpalast dresden
dresdner philharmonie   cd: arioso ARI 110/intuition (greece)
rundfunkchor prag
kinderchor prag
chor der litauischen
staatsphilharmonie
lövaas, madjarowa,
larin, emmerlich

PIOTR TCHAIKOVSKY (1840-1893)
piano concerto no 1 in b flat minor op 23
recorded on 2 march 1965 at a concert in leipzig
rsol   cd: weitblick (japan) SSS 0652
gilels

evgeny onegin, scenes from the opera
recorded in 1966 in the funkhaus nalepastrasse berlin
staatskapelle berlin   lp: eterna 820 396/825 396
croonen, burmeister,   *excerpts*
hölzke, adam, leib   lp: eterna 826 027
sung in german

GIUSEPPE VERDI (1813-1901)
messa da requiem
recorded in 1965 at a concert in leipzig
rsol   unpublished radio broadcast
rundfunkchor leipzig   *german radio archives*
landucci, casei,
bardini, cittanti

4 pezzi sacri
recorded on 6-7 december 1967 in the bethanienkirche leipzig
rsol   lp: eterna 826 088
rundfunkchor leipzig

aida, ballet music from act two
recorded in 1958 in the funkhaus leipzig
rsol   unpublished radio broadcast
                              german radio archives

verdi/morro ma prima in grazia/un ballo in maschera
recorded in 1956 in the funkhaus leipzig
rsol   unpublished radio broadcast
müller-bütow   *german radio archives*
sung in german
recorded in 1960 in the funkhaus leipzig
rsol   unpublished radio broadcast
kuhse   *german radio archives*
sung in german

o don fatale!/don carlo
recorded in 1966 in the funkhaus leipzig
rsol   unpublished radio broadcast
kehl   *german radio archives*
sung in german

spuntato ecco il di d'esultanza!/don carlo
recorded on 16 may 1952 at a concert in the kongresshalle leipzig
rsol   unpublished radio broadcast
rundfunkchor leipzig   *german radio archives*
hofer, tinschert,
horand
sung in german

la forza del destino, overture
recorded in 1960 in the funkhaus leipzig
rsol   unpublished radio broadcast
                                           german radio archives

pace pace!/la forza del destino
recorded in 1954 in the funkhaus leipzig
rsol   unpublished radio broadcast
friedland   *german radio archives*
sung in german

recorded in 1966 in the funkhaus leipzig
rsol   unpublished radio broadast
jamroz   *german radio archives*
sung in german

122

verdi/**luisa miller/**concert version for radio
recorded in 1956 in the funkhaus nalepastrasse berlin
rsob   unpublished radio broadcast
rundfunkchor berlin   *german radio archives*
wenglor, rott, stolze,
kaphahn
sung in german

macbeth/concert version for radio
recorded in 1963 in the funkhaus leipzig
rsol   unpublished radio broadcast
rundfunkchor leipzig   *german radio archives*
kehl. rose, svorc,
pietzsch
sung in german

ondine e silfidi; tre volte miagola/macbeth
recorded on 16 may 1952 at a concert in the kongresshalle leipzig
rsol   unpublished radio broadcast
rundfunkchor leipzig   *german radio archives*
sung in german

otello/concert version for radio
recorded in 1954 in the funkhaus leipzig
rsol   cd: cantus classics 500 807/
rundfunkchor leipzig   walhall WLCD 0091
friedland, walter-sacks,
miltschinoff, stolze,
löbel, roth-ehrang
sung in german

una vela!....esultate!/otello
recorded in 1951 in the funkhaus leipzig
rsol   unpublished radio broadcast
rundfunkchor leipzig   *german radio archives*
gruber
sung in german

dite alle giovine/la traviata
recorded in 1972 in the funkhaus nalepastrasse berlin
rsob   unpublished radio broadcast
casapietra   *german radio archives*

verdi/ah sio ben mio....di quella pira!/il trovatore
recorded in 1951 in the funkhaus leipzig
rsol   unpublished radio broadcast
rundfunkchor leipzig   *german radio archives*
gruber
sung in german

vedi le fosche notturne/il trovatore
recorded in 1958 in the funkhaus leipzig
rsol   unpublished radio broadcast
rundfunkchor leipzig   *german radio archives*
sung in german

ANTONIO VIVALDI (1678-1741)
sinfonia in c rv116
recorded between 30 november-3 december 1970 in the versöhnungskirche leipzig
rundfunk-   lp: eterna 826 096
kammerorchester   cd: berlin classics 02332/30532/ 32852

sinfonia in a rv160
recorded between 30 november-3 december 1970 in the versöhnungskirche leipzig
rundfunk-   cd: berlin classics 02332/93062
kammerorchester   *unpublished eterna lp recording*

sinfonia in b minor rv 169 "al santo sepolcro"
recorded between 30 november-3 december 1970 in the versöhnungskirche leipzig
rundfunk-   lp: eterna 826 096
kammerorchester   cd: berlin classics 02332/30532/ 32852

bassoon concerto in a minor rv 500
recorded between 30 november-3 december 1970 in the versöhnungskirche leipzig
rundfunk-   lp: eterna 826 096
kammerorchester   cd: berlin classics 02332/30532/ 32852
kretzschmar

124

vivaldi/**flute concerto in d rv429**

recorded between 30 november-3 december 1970 in the versöhnungskirche
leipzig

rundfunk-	lp: eterna 826 096
kammerorchester	cd: berlin classics 02332/30532/
fügner	32852

oboe concerto in d minor rv454

recorded between 30 november-3 december 1970 in the versöhnungskirche
leipzig

rundfunk-	lp: eterna 826 096
kammerorchester	cd: berlin classics 02332/30532/
schneider	32852

RICHARD WAGNER (1813-1883)

parsifal

recorded on 11 january 1975 at a concert performance in the kongresshalle
leipzig

rsol	lp: eterna 827 031-035
rundfunkchor leipzig	cd: koch 313 482/berlin classics
rundfunkchor berlin	13482
thomanerchor leipzig	*excerpts*
schröter, kollo, adam,	lp: eterna 827 036
cold, teschler, bunger	

parsifal, prelude

recorded on 30 september 1983 at a concert in tokyo

nhk symphony	cd: nhk (japan)

die meistersinger von nürnberg, overture

recorded on 26 september 1980 at a concert in tokyo

nhk symphony	cd: nhk (japan)

RUDOLF WAGNER-REGENY (1903-1969)
genesis, cantata
recorded on 27 november 1956 in the funkhaus leipzig
rsol   cd: hastedt HT 5301
rundfunkchor leipzig
töpper

die bürger von calais, scenes from the opera
recorded in 1973 in the bethanienkirche leipzig
rsol   lp: eterna 825 522
rundfunkchor leipzig
breul, bolkestein,
büchner, weimann

jüdische chronik
co-composition with blacher, dessau, hartmann and henze
see entry under miscellaneous on page 128

CARL MARIA VON WEBER (1786-1826)
abu hassan, overture
recorded in 1955 in leipzig
rsol   78: eterna 120 176

der freischütz/concert version for radio
recorded in 1965 in the funkhaus leipzig
rsol   unpublished radio broadcast
rundfunkchor leipzig   *excerpts*
croonen, schöner,   lp: eterna 860 082
gruber, klemm,   cd: ponto PO 1033
lauhöfer, adam

der freischütz, overture
recorded on 12 september 1980 at a concert in tokyo
nhk symphony   cd: nhk (japan)

weber/**kampf und sieg, cantata**
recorded in 1953 in leipzig

rsol	lp: urania (usa) URLP 7126
rundfunkchor leipzig	cd: forlane UCD 16572
schmidt-glänzsch	*forlane incorrectly dates this radio broadcast*
fleischer, lutze,	*as 1943*
krämer	

oberon/concert version for radio
recorded in 1979 in the funkhaus leipzig

rsol lp: discocorp IGI 362
trekel-burkhardt,
goldberg, neumann

ANTON VON WEBERN (1883-1945)
symphony op 21
recorded between 26-29 october 1977 in the paul-gerhardt-kirche leipzig
rsol lp: eterna 827 184/deutsche
schallplatten (japan) ET 5044
cd: berlin classics 02752/90202
sacd: avex 25292

passacaglia for orchestra op 1
recorded between 26-29 october 1977 in the paul-gerhardt-kirche leipzig
rsol lp: eterna 827 184/deutsche
schallplatten (japan) ET 5044
cd: berlin classics 01222/02752/
90202
sacd: avex 25292

five movements op 5
recorded between 26-29 october 1977 in the paul-gerhardt-kirche leipzig
rsol lp: eterna 827 184/deutsche
schallplatten (japan) ET 5044
cd: berlin classics 01222/02752/
90202
sacd: avex 25292

webern/**six pieces op 6**
recorded between 26-29 october 1977 in the paul-gerhardt-kirche leipzig
rsol   lp: eterna 827 184/deutsche
                              schallplatten (japan) ET 5044
                              cd: berlin clasics 01222/02752/90202
                              sacd: avex 25292

five pieces op 10
recorded between 26-29 october 1977 in the paul-gerhardt-kirche leipzig
rsol   lp: eterna 827 184/deutsche
                              schallplatten (japan) ET 5044
                              cd: berlin classics 01222/02752/90202
                              sacd: avex 25292

KURT WEILL (1900-1950)
die sieben todsünden, ballet with songs
recorded between 22-26 august 1966 in the heilandskirche leipzig
rsol   lp: eterna 820 732/825 732/deutsche
may, schreier, rotzsch,   grammophon 139 308/2571 124
leib, polster   cd: berlin classics 20692

MANFRED WEISS (born 1935)
organ concerto
recording date unspecified
dresdner philharmonie   lp: eterna
webersinke

GERHARD WOHLGEMUTH (1920-2001)
violin concerto
recorded on 31 august-1 september 1964 in the heilandskirche leipzig
rsol   lp: eterna 820 501/825 501/885 056
vermes

ERMANNO WOLF-FERRARI (1876-1948)
i quattro rusteghi, intermezzo
recorded in 1986 in the lukaskirche
dresdner philharmonie   lp: eterna 725 152/729 152
                              cd: capriccio 49314/laserlight 15688

HELMUT ZAPF (born 1956)
concertino for orchestra
recorded in 1988 in the funkhaus nalepastrasse berlin
staatskapelle berlin   cd: rca/bmg 74321 735092

MISCELLANEOUS
jüdische chronik
a five-movement work written in protest at anti-semitism and
composed jointly by boris blacher, paul dessau, karl amadeus
hartmann, hans werner henze and rudolf wagner-regeny
recorded on 1 april 1966 in the funkhaus leipzig

rsol	lp: eterna 820 774/825 774/
rundfunkchor leipzig	wergo 60023
barova, bauer,	cd: berlin classics 32802/90162
schall, thate	

HERBERT KEGEL AS COMPOSER
vier lieder für klavier und hohe stimme/1939-1955
performed by catherine denley (soprano) and howard arman
(piano) and included on cd accompanying the book *ein
dirigentenleben im 20. jahrhundert* (see bibliography on page 8)

Heinz Rögner 1929-2001

Born and died in Leipzig, Rögner spent the major part of his career conducting Rundfunk-Sinfonie-Orchester Leipzig (1958-1962) and Rundfunk-Sinfonie-Orchester Berlin (1973-1993). From 1984 he was also chief conductor of the Yomiuri Nippon Symphony Orchestra in Japan.

Particularly distinguished among his recordings are Bruckner Symphonies 4-9 as well as two of the Bruckner Masses, Mahler's Third Symphony and selections from the three great Tchaikovsky ballets.

PAUL ABRAHAM (1892-1960)
einmal da schlägt für uns die stunde; reich mir zum abschied noch einmal die hände/viktoria und ihr husar
recorded in 1977 in the lukaskirche

dresdner philharmonie	lp: eterna 845 047
geszty, schreier	cd: berlin classics 20922/90752

ADOLPHE ADAM (1803-1856)
ah vous dirai-je?/le toreador
recorded in 1977 in the lukaskirche

dresdner philharmonie	lp: eterna 845 061
geszty	cd: berlin classics 21432

ALEXANDER ALABIEV (1787-1851)
die nachtigall
recorded in 1977 in the lukaskirche

dresdner philharmonie	lp: eterna 845 061
geszty	cd: berlin classics 21432

TOMMASO ALBINONI (1671-1750)
trumpet concerto in b flat
recorded in april-may 1974 in berlin

kammerorchester berlin	lp: eterna 826 684/deutsche
güttler	schallplatten (japan) ET 3045

LUIGI ARDITI (1822-1903)
il bacio
recorded in 1977 in the lukaskirche

dresdner philharmonie	lp: eterna 845 061
geszty	cd: berlin classics 21432

DANIEL FRANCOIS AUBER (1782-1871)
fra diavolo, overture
recorded in 1962 in leipzig

rsol	lp: eterna 820 315/825 315

JOHANN SEBASTIAN BACH (1685-1750)
air from the third orchestral suite
televised between november-december 1991 at concerts in the suntory hall tokyo

rsob	vhs video: deutsche schallplatten (japan) TKVC 60330
	laserdisc: deutsche schallplatten (japan) TKLC 50061

LUDWIG VAN BEETHOVEN (1770-1827)
symphony no 6 in f op 68 "pastoral"
televised between november-december 1991 at concerts in the suntory hall tokyo
rsob   laserdisc: deutsche schallplatten
       (japan) TKLC 50060

symphony no 9 in d minor op 125 "choral"
televised between november-december 1991 at concerts in the suntory hall tokyo
rsob   vhs video: deutsche schallplatten
rundfunkchor berlin (japan) TKVC 60334
lampe, schwarz, laserdisc: deutsche schallplatten
rendall, polster (japan) TKLC 50065

violin concerto in d op 61
televised between november-december 1991 at concerts in the suntory hall tokyo
rsob   vhs video: deutsche schallplatten
suske   (japan) TKVC 60331
       laserdisc: deutsche schallplatten
       (japan) TKLC 50062

coriolan, overture
recorded in march 1978 in the funkhaus nalepastrasse berlin
rsob   lp: eterna 827 891
       cd: berlin classics 93402

egmont, overture
recorded in march 1978 in the funkhaus nalepastrasse berlin
rsob   lp: eterna 827 891
       cd: berlin classics 93402

fidelio, overture
recorded on 18 may 1982 in the funkhaus nalepastrasse
rsob   lp: eterna 827 890

die geschöpfe des prometheus, overture
recorded on 13 january 1982 in the funkhaus nalepastrasse berlin
rsob   lp: eterna 827 890
       cd: berlin classics 93402

televised between november-december 1991 at concerts in the suntory hall tokyo
rsob   laserdisc: deutsche schallplatten
       (japan) TKLC 50060

beethoven/**könig stephan, overture**
recording date unspecified
rsob   cd: pilz acanta 44 20732

recorded in march 1978 in the funkhaus nalepastrasse berlin
rsob   lp: eterna 827 891
                                        cd: berlin classics 93402

leonore no 1 overture
recorded on 10 june 1982 in the funkhaus nalepastrasse berlin
rsob   lp: eterna 827 890

leonore no 2 overture
recorded on 25 august 1983 in the funkhaus nalepastrasse berlin
rsob   lp: eterna 827 890

leonore no 3 overture
recorded on 26 august 1983 in the funkhaus nalepastrasse berlin
rsob   lp: eterna 827 890
                                        cd: berlin classics 93402

televised between november-december 1991 at concerts in the suntory hall tokyo
rsob   laserdisc: deutsche schallplatten
                                        (japan) TKLC 50060

die ruinen von athen, overture
recorded in march 1978 in the funkhaus nalepastrasse berlin
rsob   lp: eterna 827 891
                                        cd: berlin classics 93402

die weihe des hauses, overture
recorded in march 1978 in the funkhaus nalepastrasse berlin
rsob   lp: eterna 827 891
                                        cd: berlin classics 93402

zur namensfeier, overture
recorded in march 1978 in the funkhaus nalepastrasse berlin
rsob   lp: eterna 827 891
                                        cd: berlin classics 93402

*heinz rögner also recorded a complete beethoven symphony cycle between
1986-1994 with the yomiuri nippon symphony orchestra, precise
publication details of which could not be established*

GEORGES BIZET (1838-1975)
l'arlesienne, first and second suites from the incidental music
recorded between 2-4 january 1974 in the funkhaus nalepastrasse berlin
rsob   lp: eterna 826 623/deutsche
                             schallplatten (japan) ET 3044
                             cd: berlin classics 00182/02722/
                             32442

la jolie fille de perth, suite from the opera
recorded in may 1974 in the funkhaus nalepastrasse berlin
rsob   lp: eterna 826 623/deutsche
                             schallplatten (japan) ET 3044
                             cd: berlin classics 02722/32442

jeux d'enfants
recorded on 23-24 january 1974 in the funkhaus nalepastrasse berlin
rsob   lp: eterna 826 623/deutsche
                             schallplatten (japan) ET 3044
                             cd: berlin classics 02722/32442

LUIGI BOCCHERINI (1743-1805)
cello concerto in b flat, arranged by grützmacher
recorded in 1975 at a concert in berlin
rsob   unpublished radio broadcast
mezo   *german radio archives*

serenade in c "la musica notturna di madrid"
recorded in 1959 in the funkhaus leipzig
rundfunk-   unpublished radio broadcast
kammerorchester   *german radio archives*

JOAO DOMINGOS BOMTEMPO (1775-1842)
messa da requiem
recording date unspecified
rsob   cd: berlin classics 92452
rundfunkchor berlin
pusar, riess,
c.vogel, polster

134

JOHANNES BRAHMS (1833-1897)
symphony no 1 in c minor op 68
recorded in june 1980 in the funkhaus nalepastrasse berlin
rsob   cd: weitblick (japan) SSS 0482

symphony no 2 in d op 73
recorded on 5 may 1987 at a concert in the schauspielhaus berlin
rsob   cd: weitblick (japan) SSS 0482

recorded in november 1991 at a concert in the suntory hall tokyo
rsob   cd: deutsche schallplatten
                              (japan) TKCC 30415
                              vhs video: deutsche schallplatten
                              (japan) TKVC 60330
                              laserdisc: deutsche schallplatten
                              (japan) TKLC 50661

symphony no 3 in f op 90
recorded on 29 january 1978 at a concert in berlin
rsob   cd: weitblick (japan) SSS 0482

symphony no 4 in e minor op 98
recorded on 4 november 1978 at a concert in berlin
rsob   cd: weitblick (japan) SSS 0482

serenade no 2 in a op 16
recorded in june 1975 in the funkhaus nalepastrasse berlin
rsob   cd: pilz acanta 44 20732

academic festival overture op 80
recorded between 5-7 july 1973 in the lukaskirche
staatskapelle dresden   lp: eterna 826 560/eurodisc 201 986.250/
                              deutsche schallplatten (japan) ET 3035/
                              ET 5105

the hungarian dances, orchestral version
recorded between 5-7 july 1973 in the lukaskirche
staatskapelle dresden   lp: eterna 826 560/eurodisc 201 986.250/
                              deutsche schallplatten (japan) ET 3035/
                              ET 5105
                              numbers 4, 8, 9, 11, 14, 15 and 16 are
                              omitted from this recording

ANTON BRUCKNER (1824-1896)
symphony no 4 in e flat "romantic"
recorded between 12-16 july 1983 in the funkhaus nalepastrasse berlin

rsob

lp: eterna 827 975/amabile 014 0018/
deutsche schalplatten (japan) 22TC 278
cd: berlin classics 02172/30632
sacd: avex 25298
recording completed in january 1984

symphony no 5 in b flat
recorded between september 1983-january 1984 in the funkhaus
nalepastrasse berlin

rsob

lp: eterna 827 967-968/amabile 014 0017
cd: berlin classics 02172/30112

symphony no 6 in a
recorded between 17-19 june 1980 in the christuskirche berlin

rsob

lp: eterna 827 932/amabile 014 0015/
deutsche schallplatten (japan)
ET 5121/32TC 52
cd: berlin classics 02172/30952

symphony no 7 in e
recorded between may-august 1983 in the funkhaus nalepastrasse berlin

rsob

lp: eterna 827 880-881
cd: berlin classics 02172/30162
sacd: avex 25297

symphony no 8 in c minot
recorded between may-july 1985 in the funkhaus nalepastrasse berlin

rsob

lp: eterna 827 990-991
cd: berlin classics 02172/31182

symphony no 9 in d minor
recorded between 9-12 february 1983 in the funkhaus nalepastrasse berlin

rsob

lp: eterna 827 943/deutsche schallplatten
(japan) ET 5172/32TC 36
cd: berlin classics 02172/83782

te deum
recorded between 12-16 september 1988 in berlin

rsob
rundfunkchor berlin
hajossyova, lang,
schmidt, polster

cd: berlin clasics 2100 172/02172/
84632/92482

bruckner/**mass no 2 in e minor**
recorded between 12-16 september 1988 in berlin
rsob   lp: eterna 729 035
rundfunkchor berlin   cd: berlin classics 2100 172/02172/
                                          84632/92482

mass no 3 in f minor
recorded between 12-16 september 1988 in berkin
rsob   lp: deutsche schallplatten (japan)
rundfunkchor berlin   25TC 305
hajossyova, lang,   cd: berlin classics 2100 173/02172/
schmidt, polster   84632/92472

VICTOR BRUNS (born 1904)
violin concerto
recorded in 1969 in the funkhaus nalepastrasse berlin
rsob   lp: eterna 885 185
suske

bassoon concerto
recorded in 1969 in the funkhaus nalepastrasse berlin
rsob   lp: eterna 885 185
heilmann

MAX BUTTING (1888-1976)
piano concerto
recorded between 8-13 april 1970 in the lukaskirche
staatsksapelle dresden   lp: eterna 825 890/885 073
ander   *recording completed in june 1970*

LUIGI CHERUBINI (1760-1842)
mass in c minor
recorded on 11 october 1977 at a concert in the berliner dom
rsob   cd: pilz acanta 44 20712
rundfunkchor berlin

JOHANN CILENSEK (1913-1998)
konzertstück for violin and orchestra
recording date unspecified
rsol   lp: eterna 885 124
other

EDISON DENISOV (1929-1996)
tod ist ein langer schlaf, variations on a theme of haydn
recording date unspecified
rsol   unpublished radio broadcast
                            german radio archives

KARL DITTERS VON DITTERSDORF (1739-1799)
harp concerto in a
recorded between 11-14 july 1973 in the lukaskirche
staatskapelle dresden   lp: eterna 826 554
zoff   cd: berlin classics 2100 167

NICO DOSTAL (1895-1981)
ich bin verliebt/clivia
recorded in 1977 in the lukaskirche
dresdner philharmonie   lp: eterna 845 061
geszty   cd: berlin classics 21432

ANTONIN DVORAK (1841-1904)
symphony no 5 in f op 24
recorded in 1962 in the funkhaus leipzig
rsol   unpublished radio broadcast
                            german radio archives
violin concerto in a minor op 53
recorded in 1988 in berlin
rsob   unpublished radio broadcast
schunk   *german radio archives*
cello concerto in b minor op 104
recorded in 1975 in berlin
rsob   unpublished radio broadcast
schiff   *german radio archives*
gypsy melodies, version for mezzo-soprano and orchestra
recorded in 1978 in the funkhaus nalepastrasse berlin
rsob   unpublished radio broadcast
marova   *german radio archives*

PAUL DUKAS (1865-1935)
l'apprenti sorcier
recorded in march 1977 in berlin
rsob   lp: eterna 827 077
                        cd: berlin classics 02722/94652

HANNS EISLER (1898-1962)
kleine sinfonie (1932)
recorded in october-november 1972 in berlin
rsob   lp: eterna 885 043
                        cd: berlin classics 92332
niemandsland/second orchestral suite
recorded in october-november 1972 in berlin
rsob   lp: eterna 885 043
                        cd: berlin classics 92282
kühle wampe/third orchestral suite
recorded in october-november 1972 in berlin
rsob   lp: eterna 885 043
                        cd: berlin clasics 92282
die jugend hat das wort/fourth orchestral suite
recorded in october-november 1972 in berlin
rsob   lp: eterna 885 043
                        cd: berlin classics 92282

GEORGE ENESCU (1881-1955)
rumanian rhapsody no 1
recorded in march 1977 in berlin
rsob   lp: eterna 827 077
                        cd: berlin classics 02722/94652

MANUEL DE FALLA (1876-1946)
ritual fire dance/el amor brujo
recorded in march 1977 in berlin
rsob   lp: eterna 827 077
                        cd: berlin classics 02722/94652

JOHANN FRIEDRICH FASCH (1688-1758)
trumpet concerto in d
recorded in april-may 1974 in the funkhaus nalepastrasse berlin
kammerorchester berlin   lp: eterna 826 684/deutsche
güttler   schallplatten (japan) ET 3045

FIDELIO FRIEDRICH FINKE (1891-1968)
capriccio on a polish folksong for piano and orchestra
recorded between 8-13 april 1970 in the lukaskirche

staatskapelle dresden	lp: eterna 825 890/885 074
schorler	*recording completed in june 1970*

FRIEDRICH VON FLOTOW (1812-1883)
alessandro stradella, overture
recorded in 1959 in the funkhaus leipzig

rsol	lp: eterna 820 315

JEAN FRANCAIX (1912-1997)
jeu poetique pour harpe et orchestre
recorded between 11-14 july 1973 in the lukaskirche

staatskapelle dresden	lp: eterna 826 554
zoff	cd: berlin classics 2100 167

KARL-RUDI GRIESBACH (1916-2000)
trinke mut des reinen lebens
recorded on 21 february 1982 in the funkhaus nalepastrasse berlin

rsob	lp: eterna 885 254
lorenz	

FRANZ GROTHE (1908-1982)
mein schatz der ist der postillon/lied der nachtigall
recorded in 1977 in the lukaskirche

dresdner philharmonie	lp: eterna 845 061
geszty	cd: berlin classics 21432

GEORGE FRIDERIC HANDEL (1685-1759)
harp concerto in b flat op 4 no 6
recorded between 11-14 july 1973 in the lukaskirche

staatskapelle dresden	lp: eterna 826 554
zoff	cd: berlin classics 2100 167/93942

solomon, oratorio
recorded in june 1981 in the funkhaus nalepastrasse berlin

rsob	lp: eterna 827 731-733
rundfunkchor berlin	cd: berlin classics 21892/84682
bundschuh, schiml,	
werner, büchner,	
polster	
sung in german	

FRANZ JOSEF HAYDN (1732-1809)
oboe concerto in c
recorded between 22-24 october 1963 in the christuskirche

rsob	lp: eterna 820 428/825 428
wätzig	cd: berlin classics 01272/02722

JOHANN WILHELM HERTEL (1727-1789)
trumpet concerto in d
recorded in april-may 1974 in the funkhaus nalepastrasse berlin

kammerorchester berlin	lp: eterna 826 684/deutsche
güttler	schallplatten (japan) ET 3045

LEOS JANACEK (1854-1928)
taras bulba
recorded between 16-18 april 1980 in the christuskirche

rsob	lp: eterna 827 544/deutsche
	schallplatten (japan) ET 5113
	cd: berlin classics 02722/32422

sinfonietta
recorded on 16 november 1979 in the christuskirche

rsob	lp: eterna 827 544/deutsche
	schallplatten (japan) ET 5113
	cd: berlin classics 02722/32422

EMMERICH KALMAN (1882-1953)
die czardasfürstin, scenes from the operetta
recorded in 1969 in the lukaskirche

dresdner philharmonie	lp: eterna 845 090
rundfunkchor leipzig	cd: berlin classics 00742
rysanek, katterfeld,	
büchner, ritzmann	

EDUARD KUENNECKE (1885-1953)
ein rosenstock trägt blüten; wenn die knospen spriessen/
das dorf ohne glocke
recorded in 1977 in the lukaskirche

dresdner philharmoniw	lp: eterna 845 047
geszty, schreier	cd: berlin classics 90752

FRANZ LEHAR (1870-1948)
durch die weiten felder/wo die lerche singt
recorded in 1977 in the lukaskirche
dresdner philharmonie   lp: eterna 845 047
geszty   cd: berlin classics 20922/90752

ALBERT LORTZING (1801-1851)
holzschuhtanz/zar und zimmermann
recorded on 1 january 1987 at a concert to open the rebuilt schauspielhaus
staatskapelle berlin   lp: eterna 725 101-102

den hohen herrscher würdig zu empfangen…heil sei
dem tag!/zar und zimmermann
recorded on 1 january 1987 at a concert to open the rebuilt schauspielhaus
staatskapelle berlin   lp: eterna 725 101-102
chor der deutschen
staatsoper
vogel

regina, overture
recorded in 1990 in the funkhaus leipzig
rsol   cd: marco polo 822 0310

GUSTAV MAHLER (1860-1911)
symphony no 3 in d minor
recorded between 25-31 january 1983 in the christuskirche
rsob   lp: eterna 827 877-878
frauen- und knabenchor   cd: berlin classics 02172/21212
des berliner rundfunks   *recording completed in october 1983*
rappe

symphony no 6 in a minor
recorded between 28 january-1 february 1981 in the christuskirche
rsob   lp: eterna 827 612-613

symphony no 7 in b minor
recording date unspecified
rsob   unpublished radio broadcast
                             german radio archives

FELIX MENDELSSOHN-BARTHOLDY (1809-1947)
concerto for two pianos and orchestra
recorded in april 1972 in the funkhaus nalepastrasse berlin

rsob   lp: eterna 826 677
lejskova, legsek   cd: berlin classics 90272

violin concerto in e minor op 64
recording date unspecified

rsol   unpublished radio broadcast
weithaas   *german radio archives*

ERNST HERMANN MEYER (1905-1988)
konzertante sinfonie, for piano and orchestra
recording date unspecified

rsob   lp: eterna 885 134
zechlin

viola concerto
recorded between 8-10 december 1981 in the funkhaus leipzig

rsol   lp: eterna 885 233
lipka

GIACOMO MEYERBEER (1791-1864)
o beau pays de la touraine/les huguenots
recorded on 1 january 1987 at a concert to open the rebuilt schauspielhaus

staatskapelle berlin   lp: eterna 725 101-102
hajossyova
sung in german

DARIUS MILHAUD (1892-1974)
la creation du monde
recorded in march 1977 in the funkhaus nalepastrasse berlin

rsob   lp: eterna 827 077
                                  cd: berlin classics 02722/94652

WOLFGANG AMADEUS MOZART (1756-1791)
symphony no 30 in d k202
recorded on 25-26 june 1965 in the funkhaus leipzig
rsol   unpublished radio broadcast
                              german radio archives

piano concerto no 27 in b flat k595
recorded on 25 september 1966 at a concert in the staatsoper
staatskapelle berlin   unpublished radio broadcast
kempff   *german radio archives*

violin concerto no 5 in a k219
televised on 23 november 1991 at a concert in the suntory hall tokyo
rsob   cd: deutsche schallplatten
suske   (japan) TKCC 30417
                              vhs video: deutsche schallplatten
                              (japan) TKVC 60332
                              laserdisc: deutsche schallplatten
                              (japan) TKLC 50063

clarinet concerto in a k622
recording date unspecified
rsob   cd: pilz acanta 44 20732
rüpular

sechs deutsche tänze k536
recorded on 17 july 1967 in the funkhaus leipzig
rsol   unpublished radio broadcast
                              german radio archives

maurerische trauermusik in c minor k477
televised in december 1991 at a concert in the suntory hall tokyo
rsob   cd: deutsche schallplatten
                              (japan) TKCC 30417
                              vhs video: deutsche schallplatten
                              (japan) TKVC 60333
                              laserdisc: deutsche schallplatten
                              (japan) TKLC 50064

violin sonata in b flat k454
recorded on 6 april 1959 in the funkhaus leipzig
kovacs   unpublished radio broadcast
rögner plays the piano part   *german radio archives*

mozart/**l'amero saro costante/il re pastore**
recorded on 5 july 1969 in the funkhaus nalepastrasse berlin
rsob   unpublished radio broadcast
stolte   *german radio archives*

requiem in d minor k626
televised on 16 december 1991 at a concert in the suntory hall tokyo
rsob   cd: deutsche schallplatten
rundfunkchor berlin   (japan) TKCC 30420
lampe, schwarz,   vhs video: deutsche schallplatten
rendall, polster   (japan) TKVC 60333
                                        laserdisc: deutsche schallplatten
                                        (japan) TKLC 50064

HANS PFITZNER (1869-1949)
palestrina, the three orchestral preludes
recorded on 13-14 april 1972 in the funkhaus nalepastrasse berlin
rsob   lp: eterna 827 407

MAURICE RAVEL (1875-1937)
piano concerto in g
recorded between 11-15 november 1985 in the christuskirche
rsob   lp: eterna 828 004
arens   cd: art 3626/berlin classics
                         00842/02722

piano concerto for the left hand
recorded between 11-15 november 1985 in the christuskirche
rsob   lp: eterna 828 004
arens   cd: berlin classics 00842/02722

FRED RAYMOND (1900-1954)
schau einer schönen frau nie zu tief in die augen/maske in blau
recorded in 1977 in the lukaskirche
dresdner philharmonie   lp: eterna 845 047
schreier   cd: berlin classics 20922/90752

MAX REGER **(1873-1916)**
eine romantische suite op 125
recorded between 5-17 december 1973 in the funkhaus nalepastrasse berlin
rsob   lp: eterna 826 688
                                cd: berlin classics 02722/31192/
                                83922

sinfonischer prolog zu einer tragödie op 68/shortened version
recorded between 16-18 december 1974 in the funkhaus nalepastrasse berlin
rsob   lp: eterna 826 688
                                cd: berlin classics 02722/31192/
                                83922

NIKOLAI RIMSKY-KORSAKOV **(1844-1908)**
die südsee birgt in tiefen felsenhöhlen/sadko
recorded in 1960 in leipzig
rsol   45: eterna
neukirch

GERHARD ROSENFELD **(born 1931)**
friedensgloria für sopran, chor und orchester
recorded on 8 march 1985 in the funkhaus nalepastrasse berlin
rsob   lp: eterna 885 268
rundfunkchor berlin   cd: thorofon CTH 2344
termer

kleistbriefe
recorded on 2 february 1977 in the funkhaus nalepastrasse berlin
rsob   lp: eterna 885 160
rundfunkchor berlin

GIOACCHINO ROSSINI **(1792-1868)**
la scala di seta, overture
recorded in 1972 in berlin
rsob   cd: berlin classics 01612

CAMILLE SAINT-SAENS **(1835-1921)**
danse macabre
recorded in march 1977 in the funkhaus nalepastrasse berlin
rsob   lp: eterna 827 077
                                cd: berlin classics 02722/94652

ARNOLD SCHOENBERG (1874-1951)
orchestral variations op 31
recorded on 4 april 1989 at a concert in leipzig
rsol   cd: weitblick (japan) SSS 0482

verklärte nacht, orchestral version
recorded on 10 november 1991 at a concert in berlin
rsob   cd: weitblick (japan) SSS 0482

five orchestral pieces op 16
recorded on 14 january 1980 at a concert in berlin
rsob   cd: weitblick (japan) SSS 0482

pelleas und melisande op 5
recorded on 10 february 1987 at a concert in leipzig
rsob   cd: weitblick (japan) SSS 0482

kammersinfonie no 1
recorded on 3 march 1989 at a concert in berlin
rsob   cd: weitblick (japan) SSS 0482

kammersinfonie no 2
recorded on 29 september 1987 at a concert in leipzig
rsob   cd: weitblick (japan) SSS 0482

FRANZ SCHUBERT (1797-1828)
symphony no 2 in b flat d125
recording date unspecified
rsob   cd: pilz acanta 44 20722

symphony no 6 in c d589
recording date unspecified
rsob   cd: pilz acanta 44 20722

symphony no 9 in c d944 "great"
recorded between 10-14 june 1978 in the christuskirche
rsob   lp: eterna 827 291/denon
                                        OB 7350-7351
                                        cd: denon C37 7060/CO 41552/
                                        COCO 85023

schubert/**symphonic fragments d729, arranged by weingartner**
recorded between 30 march-1 april 1977 in the funkhaus nalepastrasse berlin
rsob   lp: deutsche schallplatten (japan) ET 5031
                                       cd: berlin classics 83762/deutsche
                                       schallplatten (japan) 32TC 115

overture in b flat d470
recording date unspecified
rsob   cd: pilz acanta 44 20722

overture in d d556
recording date unspecified
rsob   cd: pilz acanta 44 20722

MANFRED SCHUBERT (born 1937)
cantilena e capriccio
recorded in february 1978 in the funkhaus nalepastrasse berlin
rsob   lp: eterna 885 108

JEAN SIBELIUS (1865-1957)
violin concerto in d minor op 47
recording date unspecified
rsol   unpublished radio broadcast
tretjakov   *german radio archives*

LEO SPIES (1889-1965)
friedenslied/friede auf unserer erde
recorded in 1960 in berlin
rsob   lp: eterna 815 045
vogel

ROBERT STOLZ (1880-1975)
zwei herzen im dreivierteltakt/der verlorene walzer
recorded in 1977 in the lukaskirche
dresdner philharmonie   lp: eterna 845 047
geszty, schreier   cd: berlin classics 20922/90752

JOHANN STRAUSS II (1825-1899)

mein herr marquis!; spiel' ich die unschuld vom lande/ die fledermaus
recorded in 1977 in the lukaskirche
dresdner philharmonie   lp: eterna 845 061
geszty   cd: berlin classics 21432

frühlingsstimmen, waltz
recorded in 1977 in the lukaskirche
dresdner philharmonie   lp: eterna 845 061
geszty   cd: berlin classics 21432

eine nacht in venedig, scenes from the operetta
recorded in 1969 in the lukaskirche
dresdner philharmonie   lp: eterna 845 069
rundfunkchor leipzig   cd: berlin classics 00772/02722
ebert, katterfeld,
rönisch, ritzmann,
neukirch, vogel, süss

seid umschlungen, waltz
recorded in 1961 in the funkhaus leipzig
rsol   unpublished radio broadcast
                            german radio archives

der zigeunerbaron, scenes from the operetta
recorded between 21-24 november 1967 in haus auensee leipzig
rsol   lp: eterna 820 817/825 817
rundfunkchor leipzig   cd: berlin classics 00772/02722
ebert, katterfeld,
ritzmann, hölzke,
hellmich, krämer

RICHARD STRAUSS (1864-1949)
grossmächtige prinzessin/ariadne auf naxos
recorded in 1974 in the funkhaus nalepastrasse berlin
rsob   unpublished radio broadcast
nawe   *german radio archives*

burleske for piano and orchestra
recorded in 1984 in the funkhaus nalepastrasse berlin
rsob   unpublished radio broadcast
rösel   *german radio archives*

duett-concertino for clarinet, bassoon and orchestra
recorded on 22-23 april 1965 in the funkhaus nalepastrasse berlin
rsob   lp: eterna 820 550/825 550
michallik, buttkewitz

was wollt ihr hier?/die frau ohne schatten
recorded in 1969 in the funkhaus leipzig
rsol   unpublished radio broadast
ziese, stilo   *german radio archives*

horn concerto no 1
recorded between 30 march-3 april 1970 in the lukaskirche
staatskapelle dresden   lp: eterna 825 883/eurodisc
damm   PK 80735
                        cd: berin classics 91802

horn concerto no 2
recorded between 30 march-3 april 1970 in the lukaskirche
staatskapelle dresden   lp: eterna 825 883/eurodisc
damm   PK 80735
                        cd: berlin classics 91802

oboe concerto
recorded between 22-24 october 1963 in the christuskirche
rsob   lp: eterna 820 428/825 428
wätzig   cd: berlin classics 01272/02722

richard strauss/**der rosenkavalier, waltz sequences**
recorded between 1-8 february 1977 in the funkhaus nalepastrasse berlin
rsob   lp: deutsche schallplatten
                                  (japan) ET 5008
                                  cd: berlin classics 02722
                                  sacd: avex 25296

salome, dance of the seven veils
recorded between 1-8 february 1977 in the funkhaus nalepastrasse berlin
rsob   lp: deutsche schallplatten
                                  (japan) ET 5008
                                  cd: berlin classics 02722
                                  sacd: avex 25296

violin concerto
recorded in 1967 in the funkhaus leipzig
rsol   unpublished radio broadcast
garay   *german radio archives*

HEINRICH SUTERMEISTER (1910-1995)
messa da requiem
recorded in 1991 in the funkhaus nalepastrasse berlin
rsob   cd: wergo 62942
rundfunkchor berlin
orgonasova, trekel

te deum
recorded in 1991 in the funkhaus nalepastrasse berlin
rsob   cd: wergo 62942
rundfunkchor berlin
orgonasova

PIOTR TCHAIKOVSKY (1840-1893)
casse noisette, selection from the ballet
comprises more extensive extracts than the standard ballet suite
recorded between 24-26 august 1982 in the funkhaus nalepastrasse berlin
rsob   lp: eterna 827 673
                             cd: berlin classics 00252/02722/
                             31162
                             recording completed in november 1982

sleeping beauty, selection from the ballet
comprises more extensive extracts than the standard ballet suite
recorded on 8 april 1980 in the christuskirche
rsob   lp: eterna 827 510/deutsche
                             schallplatten (japan) ET 5126
                             cd: berlin classics 00702/02722/
                             31162
                             recording completed in november 1980

swan lake, selection from the ballet
comprises more extensive extracts than the standard ballet suite
recorded between 18-25 november 1981 in the funkhaus nalepastrasse berlin
rsob   lp: eterna 827 662
                             cd: berlin classics 00712/02722/
                             31162/32412

GEORG PHILIPP TELEMANN (1681-1767)
die hoffnung sei mein leben, cantata for bass and strings
recorded on 7 february 1975 in the christuskirche
kammerorchester berlin   lp: eterna 827 373
süss   cd: berlin classics 91352

der kanarienvogel, cantata for bass and orchestra
recorded on 7 february 1975 in the christuskirche
kammerorchester berlin   lp: eterna 827 373
süss   cd: berlin classics 91352

der schulmeister, cantata for bass, boys' choir and strings
recorded on 7 february 1975 in the christuskirche
kammerorchester berlin   lp: eterna 827 373
thomanerchor leipzig   cd: berlin classics 84462/91352/
süss   94672

MIKIS THEODORAKIS (born 1925)
symphony no 3
recorded on 29 april 1982 at a concert in the komische oper berlin
orchester der   lp: eterna 827 739-740
komischen oper   cd: berlin classics 02802/32412
rundfunkchor berlin
bolkenstein

GIUSEPPE TORELLI (1658-1709)
trumpet concerto in d
recorded in april-may 1974 in the funkhaus nalepastrasse berlin
kammerorchester berlin   lp: eterna 826 684/deutsche
güttler   schallplatten (japan) ET 3045

RICHARD WAGNER (1813-1883)
symphony in c
recorded between 31 october-4 november 1978 in the christuskirche
rsob   lp: eterna 827 441/deutsche
                                        schallplatten (japan) ET 5073
                                        cd: berlin classics 02172/94082

siegfried idyll
recorded between 31 october-4 november 1978 in the christuskirche
rsob   lp: eterna 827 441/deutsche
                                        schallplatten (japan) ET 5073
                                        cd: berlin classics 02172/94082

die meistersinger von nürnberg, overture
recorded between 1-8 february 1977 in the christuskirche
rsob   lp: deutsche schallplatten (japan) ET 5008
                                        cd: berlin classics 02722
                                        sacd: avex 25296

das rheingold, prelude
recorded between 1-8 february 1977 in the christuskirche
rsob   lp: deutsche schallplatten (japan) ET 5008
                                        cd: berlin classics 02722
                                        sacd: avex 25296

tristan und isolde, prelude with concert ending
recorded between 1-8 february 1977 in the christuskirche
rsob   lp: deutsche schallplatten (japan) ET 5008
                                        cd: berlin classics 02722
                                        sacd: avex 5296

heinz rögner also recorded various wagner orchestral pieces with the yomiuri
nippon symphony orchestra at concerts in tokyo between 1990-1994,
precise publication details of which could not be established

FRIEDRICH WANEK (1929-1991)
tableau symphonique for orchestra
recorded in 1991 in berlin
rsob   cd: wergo 62082
musique concertante for two harpsichords and small orchestra
recorded in 1991 in berlin
rsob   cd: wergo 62082
kiss, martin
due sonetti for mezzo-soprano and strings
recorded in 1991 in berlin
rsob   cd: wergo 62082
naidu

CARL MARIA VON WEBER (1786-1826)
abu hassan
recorded between 5-10 february 1971 in the lukaskirche
staatskapelle dresden   lp: eterna 826 131/eurodisc
chor der staatsoper   92959/MR 80680
dresden   cd: rca/bmg 74321 405772
hallstein, schreier,   *excerpts*
adam   lp: eurodisc 302 203.420
abu hassan, overture
recorded in 1955 in the funkhaus leipzig
rsol   78: eterna 120 176

KURT WEILL (1900-1950)
gisela may sings brecht songs from mahagonny, threepenny opera and happy end
recorded on 26 november 1965 in the funkhaus nalepastrasse berlin
studio-orchester   lp: eterna 820 427/825 427
männerchor   cd: berlin classics 20692
may   *recordings completed in december 1965*

GERHARD WINKLER (1906-1977)
komm casanova küss mich!/casanova-lied
recorded in 1977 in the lukaskirche
dresdner philharmonie   lp: eterna 845 061
geszty   cd: berlin classics 20922/21432

ERMANNO WOLF-FERRARI (1876-1948)
serenade for strings
recorded between december 1975-february 1976 in the christuskirche
rsob   lp: eterna 826 880/deutsche
schallplatten (japan) ET 3071
cd: berlin classics 02722/91772

il campanello, prelude, intermezzo and ritornello
recorded between december 1975-february 1976 in the christuskirche
rsob   lp: eterna 826 880/deutsche
schallplatten (japan) ET 3071
cd: berlin classics 02722/91772

le donne curiosi, overture
recorded between december 1975-february 1976 in the christuskirche
rsob   lp: eterna 826 880/deutsche
schallplatten (japan) ET 3071
cd: berlin classics 02722/91772

i gioielli della madonna, neapolitan dance
recorded between december 1975-february 1976 in the christuskirche
rsob   lp: eterna 826 880/deutsche
schallplatten (japan) ET 3071
cd: berlin classics 02722/91772/
art 185232

i quatro rusteghi, intermezzo
recorded between december 1975-february 1976 in the christuskirche
rsob   lp: eterna 826 880/deutsche
schallplatten (japan) ET 3071
cd: berlin classics 02722/91772

il segreto di susanna, overture
recorded between december 1975-february 1976 in the christuskirche
rsob   lp: eterna 826 880/deutsche
schallplatten (japan) ET 3071
cd: berlin classics 02722/91772

MISCELLANEOUS
theo adam singt barock-arien
recorded between december 1975-february 1976 in the funkhaus nalepastrasse berlin

| kammerorchester berlin | lp: eterna 826 896/deutsche schallplatten |
| adam | (japan) ET 5010/ET 5040 |

reiner süss singt komische opernszenen von cimarosa, dittersdorf, hasse and lortzing
recorded between 4-8 february 1975 in the christuskirche

rsob	lp: eterna 826 871
rundfunkchor berlin	cd: berlin classics 94672
süss	

tausend rote rosen blühn: melodies by friml, böhm, kattnigg, leoncavallo, liszt, raymond, schubert, tauber, capua, curtis, klein, masanetz, meisel, spoliansky and winkler
recored in 1977 in the lukaskirche

| dresdner philharmonie | lp: eterna/decca (germany) 621 549AS |
| schreier | |

wartburg-konzert
recording date and contents unspecified

| kammerorchester berlin | lp: eterna 827 409 |
| schreier | |

Heinz Bongartz 1894-1978

After studies in his home town Krefeld, as well as Cologne and Berlin,
Heinz Bongartz was supported by the Brahms disciple Fritz Steinbach
and subsequently undertook provincial opera engagements in Kassel
and Saarbrücken. Early orchestral work included concerts with the
renowned Meiningen orchestra.

Bongartz was chief conductor of Dresden's second orchestra, the
Dresdner Philharmonie, from 1947 until 1964, but continued guest
conducting until shortly before his death in that city. Outstanding
among his recordings are the two orchestral serenades of Brahms
and a number of major works by Max Reger, as well as a set of
Beethoven's incidental music for Goethe's *Egmont*.

JOHANN SEBASTIAN BACH (1685-1750)
recordings of the second and fifth brandenburg concertos by bongartz with
the leipzig gewandhaus orchestra, mentioned by john holmes in
conductors on record, could not be verified

LUDWIG VAN BEETHOVEN (1770-1827)
symphony no 3 in e flat op 55 "eroica"
recorded on 9 november 1977 at a concert in the kulturpalast dresden
dresdner philharmonie   cd: weitblick (japan) SSS 0542

piano concerto no 1 in c op 15
recorded on 26-27 november 1958 in the hygienemuseum dresden
dresdner philharmonie   lp: eterna 820 064
zechlin

rondo for piano and orchestra wo06
recorded between 6-10 april 1970 in the versöhnungskirche leipzig
gewandhaus-orchester   lp: eterna 826 121
rösel   cd: berlin classics 20782/93092

violin romance no 1 in g op 40
recorded between 6-10 april 1970 in the versöhnungskirche leipzig
gewandhaus-orchester   lp: eterna 826 121
suske   cd: berlin classics 20782/93092/
      art 3671

violin romance no 2 in f op 60
recorded between 6-10 april 1970 in the versöhnungskirche leipzig
gewandhaus-orchester   lp: eterna 826 121
suske   cd: berlin classics 20782/93092

konzertsatz for violin and orchestra wo05
recorded between 6-10 april 1970 in the versöhnungskirche leipzig
gewandhaus-orchester   lp: eterna 826 121
suske   cd: berlin classics 20782/93092

beethoven/**egmont, incidental music to goethe's play**
recorded between 6-10 july 1970 in the christuskirche

staatskapelle berlin	lp: eterna 825 700/deutsche
breul, schulze	schallplatten (japan) ET 3056
	cd: berlin classics 91062

wellingtons sieg
recorded between 1-3 july 1970 in the christuskirche

rsob	lp: eterna 826 182
	cd: berlin classics 20782

HEINZ BONGARTZ (1894-1978)
patria o muerte, dedicated to fidel castro and the
cuban people
reording date unspecified

dresdner philharmonie	lp: eterna

JOHANNES BRAHMS (1833-1897)
serenade no 1 in d op 11
recorded between 16-20 may 1960 in the lukaskirche

dresdner philharmonie	lp: eterna 820 209/825 209/825 484
	cd: berlin classics 02632/13592/
	90232

serenade no 2 in a op 16
recorded between 5-7 april 1961 in the lukaskirche

dresdner philharmonie	lp: eterna 720 155/826 425/
	deutsche grammophon 135 138
	cd: berlin classics 02482/13592/
	90192

tragic overture op 81
recorded on 12 march 1972 in the lukaskirche

dresdner philharmonie	lp: eterna 826 425

alto rhapsody op 53
recorded between 12-14 february 1968 in the heilandskirche leipzig

rsol	lp: eterna 825 994
rundfunkchor leipzig	cd: berlin classics 31402
burmeister	*recording completed in may 1968*

ANTON BRUCKNER (1824-1896)
symphony no 6 in a
recorded between 14-16 december 1964 in the heilandskirche leipzig
gewandhaus-orchester   lp: eterna 825 540-541/philips
                         835 388AY/philips (usa) PHC 9048
                         cd: berlin classics 91672

JOHANN CILENSEK (1913-1998)
symphony no 1
recorded on 29-30 november 1958 in the funkhaus nalepastrasse berlin
rsob   lp: eterna 820 065/885 148

ANTONIN DVORAK (1841-1904)
symphony no 7 in d minor op 70
recorded in december 1962 in the lukaskirche
dresdner philharmonie   lp: eterna 720 191/825 828/
                         electrola E 91328/STE 91328
                         cd: berlin classics 02482/90192

FIDELIO FRIEDRICH FINKE (1891-1968)
orchestral suite no 3
recorded between 27-29 november 1961 in the lukaskirche
dresdner philharmonie   lp: eterna 720 165/820 487/
                         825 487/885 074

FRANZ JOSEF HAYDN (1732-1809)
symphony no 94 in g "surprise"
recorded on 21 september 1954 in the hygienemuseum dresden
dresdner philharmonie   lp: eterna 720 004

PAUL HINDEMITH (1895-1963)
nobilissima visione
recorded between 9-11 october 1963 in the lukaskirche
dresdner philharmonie   lp: eterna 820 484/825 484/
                         wergo 60027
                         cd: berlin classics 00962/30412

mathis der maler, symphony
recorded between 14-17 october 1963 in the lukaskirche
dresdner philharmonie   lp: eterna 720 199/825 870

160

WOLFGANG HOHENSEE (born 1927)
konzertante ouvertüre
recorded between 14-17 march 1966 in the lukaskirche
dresdner philharmonie   lp: eterna 825 668

SIEGFRIED KURZ (born 1930)
sinfonia piccola
recorded between 14-17 march 1966 in the lukaskirche
dresdner philharmonie   lp: eterna 825 668

trumpet concerto
recorded on 20-21 january 1958 in the funkhaus nalepastrasse berlin
dresdner philharmonie   lp: eterna 820 065
stephan

FRANZ LISZT (1811-1886)
piano concerto no 1
recorded on 24-25 march 1959 in the bethanienkirche leipzig
rsol   lp: eterna 720 090
w.richter

HORST LOHSE (born 1943)
divertimento for strings
recorded between 14-17 march 1966 in the lukaskirche
dresdner philharmonie   lp: eterna 820 668/825 668

GUSTAV MAHLER (1860-1911)
symphony no 6 in a minor
recorded on 30 june 1969 in the bethanienkirche leipzig
rsol   cd: weitblick (japan) SSS 0532

**rückert-lieder: ich atmet einen linden duft; um mitternacht;
ich bin der welt abhanden gekommen**
recorded between 9-13 september 1968 in the bethanienkirche leipzig
rsol   lp: eterna 825 994
burmeister

WOLFGANG AMADEUS MOZART (1756-1791)
symphony no 36 in c k425 "linz"
recorded on 14 december 1965 at a concert in the kongresshalle leipzig
rsol   unpublished radio broadcast
                                  german radio archives

piano concerto no 26 in d k537 "coronation"
recorded between 6-9 september 1960 in the lukaskirche
dresdner philharmonie   lp: eterna 720 135
webersinke

NICCOLO PAGANINI (1782-1840)
violin concerto no 1 in d op 6
recorded between 7-10 january 1963 in the lukaskirche
dresdner philharmonie   lp: eterna 720 179/825 840
voicu   cd: berlin classics 32402

SERGEI PROKOFIEV (1891-1953)
piano concerto no 2 in g minor op 16
recorded in november 1969 in leipzig
rsol   lp: eterna 825 895
rösel   cd: berlin classics 01072

violin concerto no 2 in g minor op 63
recorded on 9-10 january 1963 in the lukaskirche
dresdner philharmonie   lp: eterna 820 381/825 381/deutsche
voicu   grammophon 89 786

SERGEI RACHMANINOV (1873-1943)
rhapsody on a theme of paganini
recorded between 2-5 april 1963 in the bethanienkirche leipzig
rsol   lp: eterna 820 392/825 392
sak

MAX REGER (1873-1916)

sinfonietta op 90

recorded on 24 april 1966 in the sendesaal cologne

sinfonieorchester des   lp: garnet G 40140
westdeutschen rundfunks

recorded between 13-16 november 1972 in the lukaskirche

dresdner philharmonie   lp: eterna 826 396
                                   cd: berlin classics 32232/83992/91222

sinfonischer prolog zu einer tragödie op 108/shortened version

recorded on 24 april 1966 in the sendesaal cologne

sinfonieorchester des   unpublished radio broadcast
westdeutschen rundfunks   *german radio archives*

vier tondichtungen für orchester nach arnold böcklin op 128: der geigende eremit; im spiel der wellen; die toteninsel; bacchanal

recorded between 15-17 june 1964 in the lukaskirche

dresdner philharmonie   lp: eterna 820 484/825 484
                                   cd: berlin classics 21772/83992

variationen und fuge über ein thema von mozart op 132

recorded between 26-29 august 1968 in the lukaskirche

staatskapelle dresden   lp: eterna 826 063
                                   cd: berlin classics 21772/83992/93942

an die hoffnung op 124

recorded between 12-14 february 1968 in the heilandskirche leipzig

rsol   lp: eterna 825 994
burmeister   cd: berlin classics 32232/83992/91222

hymnus der liebe op 136

recorded on 24 april 1966 in the sendesaal cologne

sinfonieorchester des   unpublished radio broadcast
westdeutschen rundfunks   *german radio archives*
burmeister

recorded between 12-14 february 1968 in the heilandskirche leipzig

rsol   lp: eterna 825 994
burmeister   cd: berlin blassics 32232/83992/91222

GIOACCHINO ROSSINI (1792-1968)
guilleaume tell, overture
recorded in the hygienemuseum dresden
dresdner philharmonie   78: eterna 204 079-080
                               45: eterna 520 061

PABLO DE SARASATE (1844-1908)
zigeunerweisen for violin and orchestra
recorded between 7-10 january 1963 in the lukaskirche
dresdner philharmonie   lp: eterna 825 840
voicu   cd: berlin classics 32402/art 3657

JEAN SIBELIUS (1865-1957)
finlandia op 26
recorded on 10-11 may 1962 in the lukaskirche
dresdner philharmonie   lp: eterna 720 172/825 828
                               cd: berlin classics 02632/90232/
                               art 3658

valse triste op 44
recorded on 10-11 may 1962 in the lukaskirche
dresdner philharmonie   lp: eterna 825 828
                               cd: berlin classics 02632/90232/
                               art 3657

RICHARD STRAUSS (1864-1949)
burleske for piano and orchestra
recorded on 23-24 september 1959 in the bethanienkirche leipzig
rsol   lp: eterna 720 090
w.richter

don juan
recorded on 5 february 1977 at a concert in the kulturpalast dresden
dresdner philharmonie   cd: weitblick (japan) SSS 0542

ein heldenleben
recorded in 1965 at a concert in the kongresshalle leipzig
rsol   unpublished radio broadcast
                               german radio archives

PIOTR TCHAIKOVSKY (1840-1893)
piano concerto no 2 in g op 44
recorded on 21-22 november 1961 in the lukaskirche
dresdner philharmonie   lp: eterna 820 334/825 334
w.richter

JOHANNES PAUL THILMAN (1906-1973)
symphony no 4
recorded between 25-28 november 1959 in the lukaskirche
dresdner philharmonie   lp: eterna 820 149/825 149

piccola partita for orchestra
recorded between 14-17 march 1966 in the lukaskirche
dresdner philharmonie   lp: eterna 825 668
                             cd: rca/bmg 74321 735142

CARL MARIA VON WEBER (1786-1826)
oberon overture
recorded on 17 january 1955 in the hygienemuseum dresden
dresdner philharmonie   lp: eterna 720 028

Helmut Koch 1908-1975

Koch's early studies in Essen and Cologne with, among others, Max
Fiedler and Fritz Lehmann, were followed by an extensive period
of tutelage as a choral trainer under Hermann Scherchen. His
practical activities were interrupted by the Second World War,
for the duration of which Koch worked as a recording supervisor
for the Kristall and Odeon companies. His competence in the
technical matters of recording stood him in good stead when he
assumed administrative responsibilities both for Radio DDR
and later VEB Deutsche Schallplatten (Eterna). After founding
the Kammerorchester Berlin (from members of both the
Staatskapelle and the Berlin Rundfunk-Sinfonie-Orchester),
Koch also created and trained professional choirs known as
Solistenvereinigung des Deutschlandsenders and Grosser Chor
des Berliner Rundfunks, with which he performed important
choral works of the Baroque and Classical periods, becoming
in particular an expert and champion of the works of Handel.

Helmut Koch also worked closely with the DDR administration
in championing modern music (Eisler and Shostakovich are
good examples) and pieces which conformed to the cultural
ideals of the Socialist state.

ANATOLI ALEXANDROV (1888-1982)
hymn of the soviet socialist republics
recording date unspecified
grosser chor und   45: eterna 410 118
solistenvereinigung des
deutschlandsenders

CARL PHILIPP EMANUEL BACH (1714-1788)
sinfonia in d h663
recorded between 7-11 july 1969 in the christuskirche
kammerorchester berlin   lp: eterna 825 923/deutsche
                              schallplatten (japan) CT 2021
                              cd: berlin classics 91472
                              recording completed in september 1969

sinfonia in e flat h664
recorded between 7-11 july 1969 in the christuskirche
kammerorchester berlin   lp: eterna 825 923/deutsche
                              schallplatten (japan) CT 2021
                              cd: berlin classics 91472
                              recording completed in september 1969

sinfonia in f h665
recorded between 7-11 july 1969 in the christuskirche
kammerorchester berlin   lp: eterna 825 923/deutsche
                              schallplatten (japan) CT 2021
                              cd: berlin classics 91472
                              recording completed in september 1969

sinfonia in g h666
recorded between 7-11 july 1969 in the christuskirche
kammerorchester berlin   lp: eterna 825 923/deutsche
                              schallplatten (japan) CT 2021
                              cd: berlin clasics 91472
                              recording completed in september 1969

JOHANN CHRISTIAN BACH (1735-1782)
sinfonia in g minor t264 no 6
recorded between 2-8 february 1971 in the christuskirche
kammerorchester berlin   lp: eterna 826 194
                                              cd: berlin classics 92582

sinfonia in e flat t268 no 2
recorded between 2-8 february 1971 in the christuskirche
kammerorchester berlin   lp: eterna 720 047/826 194
                                              cd: berlin classics 18692/18732/
                                              92582

sinfonia in b flat/overture to lucio silla
recorded between 2-8 february 1971 in the christuskirche
kammerorchester berlin   45: eterna 520 115
                                              lp: eterna 720 047/826 194
                                              cd: berlin classics 18692/18732/
                                              92582

sinfonia in d/overture to amadis de gaule
recorded between 2-8 february 1971 in the christuskirhe
kammerorchester berlin   lp: eterna 826 194
                                              cd: berlin classics 92582

JOHANN SEBASTIAN BACH (1685-1750)
brandenburg concerto no 1 in f bwv1046
recorded on 29 april 1963 in the bethanienkirche leipzig
gewandhaus-orchester   lp: eterna 820 341-342/825 341-342
                                              recording completed in may and june 1963

recorded between 17-27 june 1970 in the funkhaus nalepastrasse berlin
kammerorchester berlin   lp: eterna 826 566-567/deutsche
                                              schallplatten (japan) ET 3069-3070
                                              cd: berlin classics 02542/18662/
                                              18672/29242

bach/**brandenburg concerto no 2 in f bwv1047**
recorded on 29 april 1963 in the bethanienkirche leipzig

gewandhaus-orchester	lp: eterna 820 341-342/820 371/ 825 341-342/825 371 *recording completed in may and june 1963*

recorded between 17-27 june 1970 in the funkhaus nalepastrasse berlin

kammerorchester berlin	lp: eterna 826 566-567/deutsche schallplatten (japan) ET 3069-3070 cd: berlin classics 02542/18662/ 18675/29242

brandenburg concerto no 3 in g bwv1048
recorded on 29 april 1963 in the bethanienkirche leipzig

gewandhaus-orchester	45: eterna 520 283 lp: eterna 820 341-342/820 371/ 825 341-342/825 371 *recording completed in may and june 1963*

recorded between 17-27 june 1970 in the funkhaus nalepastrasse berlin

kammerorchester berlin	lp: eterna 826 566-567/deutsche schallplatten (japan) ET 3069-3070 cd: berlin classics 02542/18662/ 18675/29242

brandenburg concerto no 4 in g bwv1049
recorded on 29 april 1963 in the bethanienkirche leipzig

gewandhaus-orchester	lp: eterna 820 341-342/825 341-342 *recording completed in may and june 1963*

recorded between 17-27 june 1970 in the funkhaus nalepastrasse berlin

kammerorchester berlin	lp: eterna 826 566-567/deutsche schallplatten (japan) ET 3069-3070 cd: berlin classics 02552/18652/ 18672/29242

bach/**brandenburg concerto no 5 in d bwv1050**
recorded on 29 april 1963 in the bethanienkirche leipzig

gewandhaus-orchester	lp: eterna 820 341-342/820 371/ 825 341-342/825 371
	recording completed in may and june 1963

recorded between 17-27 june 1970 in the funkhaus nalepastrasse berlin

kammerorchester berlin	lp: eterna 826 566-567/deutsche schallplatten (japan) ET 3069-3070
	cd: berlin classics 02552/18652/ 18672/29242

brandenburg concerto no 6 in b flat bwv1051
recorded on 29 april 1963 in the bethanienkirche leipzig

gewandhaus-orchester	lp: eterna 820 341-342/825 341-342
	recording completed in may and june 1963

recorded between 17-27 june 1970 in the funkhaus nalepastrasse berlin

kammerorchester berlin	lp: eterna 826 566-567/deutsche schallplatten (japan) ET 3069-3070
	cd: berlin classics 02552/18652/ 18672/29242

keyboard concerto in d minor bwv1052
recorded on 15 december 1957 in the funkhaus nalepastrasse berlin

kammerorchester berlin	lp: eterna 820 036
pischner	

concerto in a minor for flute, violin and harpsichord bwv1044
recorded on 15 december 1957 in the funkhaus nalepastrasse berlin

kammerorchester berlin	lp: eterna 820 036
milzkott, michailov, pischner	

orchestral suite no 1 in c bwv1066
recorded between 26 january-5 february 1965 in the heilandskirche leipzig

gewandhaus-orchester	lp: eterna 820 511-512/825 511-512

recorded in 1973-1974 in the funkhaus nalepastrasse berlin

kammerorchester berlin	lp: eterna 826 568-569/deutsche schallplatten (japan) ET 3010-3011
	cd: berlin classics 02562/18662/ 18672

bach/**orchestral suite no 2 in b minor bwv1067**
recorded between 26 january-5 february 1965 in the heilandskirche leipzig
gewandhaus-orchester   lp: eterna 820 511-512/825 511-512

recorded on 8 december 1973 in the funkhaus nalepastrasse berlin
kammerorchester berlin   lp: eterna 826 568-569/deutsche
                                  schallplatten (japan) ET 3010-3011
                                  cd: berlin classics 00452/02562/
                                  18662/18672/art 3611

orchestral suite no 3 in d bwv1068
recorded between 26 january-5 february 1965 in the heilandskirche leipzig
gewandhaus-orchester   lp: eterna 820 511-512/825 511-512
                                  air only
                             lp: eterna 810 037

recorded in 1973-1974 in the funkhaus nalepastrasse berlin
kammerorchester berlin   lp: eterna 826 568-569/deutsche
                                  schallplatten (japan) ET 3010-3011
                                  cd: berlin classics 00452/02562/
                                  18662/18672/art 3611

orchestral suite no 4 in d bwv1068
recorded between 26 january-5 february 1965 in the heilandskirche leipzig
gewandhaus-orchester   lp: eterna 820 511-512/825 511-512

recorded in 1973-1974 in the funkhaus nalepastrasse berlin
kammerorchester berlin   lp: eterna 826 568-569/deutsche
                                  schallplatten (japan) ET 3010-3011
                                  cd: berlin classics 00452/18662/
                                  18672

cantata no 202 "weichet nur betrübte schatten"
recorded on 1 april 1959 in the funkhaus nalepastrasse berlin
kammerorchester berlin   lp: eterna 820 157/825 157
vulpius

bach/**cantata no 205 "der zufriedengestellte äolus"**
recorded between 19-30 january 1951 in the haus des rundfunks
masurenallee berlin

kammerorchester berlin   unpublished radio broadcast
solistenvereinigung   *german radio archives*
des deutschlandsenders
schlemm, eustrati,
lutze, wolfram
recorded between september 1973-march 1974 in the christuskirche
kammerorchester berlin   lp: eterna 826 582
rundfunkchor berlin

cantata no 206 "schleicht spielende wellen"
recorded between september 1973-march 1974 in the christuskirche
kammerorchester berlin   lp: eterna 826 583
rundfunkchor berlin

cantata no 208 "was mir behagt ist die munt're jagd"
recorded in 1969 in the funkhaus nalepastrasse berlin
kammerorchester berlin   unpublished radio broadcast
schreier   *german radio archives*

LUDWIG VAN BEETHOVEN (1770-1827)
christus am ölberge, oratorio op 85
recorded in december 1969 in the funkhaus nalepastrasse berlin
rsob   lp: eterna 826 132
solistenvereinigung   cd: berlin classics 02682/91322
des deutschlandsenders
geszty, reti, polster
cantata on the death of emperor joseph II woo87
recorded between 20-22 may 1970 in the funkhaus nalepastrasse berlin
rsob   lp: eterna 826 258/chant du
rundfunkchor leipzig   monde LDX 8059
laux, münzing,   *recording completed in june 1970*
kühnert, schwerdegger
meeresstille und glückliche fahrt, cantata op 112
recorded between 16-27 june 1969 in the christuskirche
rsob   lp: eterna 826 258
rundfunkchor berlin   cd: berlin classics 02682/32022/
                            32392/art 5971

beethoven/**wo sich die pulse jugendlich schlagen/die weihe des hauses woo98**
recorded betveen 16-27 june 1969 in the christuskirche

rsob	lp: eterna 826 258
rundfunkchor berlin	cd: berlin classics 02682/32022/
vulpius	32392

musik zu einem ritterballett woo1
recording date unspecified

rsob	lp: urania (usa) 7111

twelve german dances woo8
recorded between 19-25 august 1969 in the funkhaus nalepastrasse berlin

kammerorchester berlin	lp: eterna 826 066
	cd: berlin classics 02682/91312

twelve contredanses woo14
recorded between 19-25 august 1969 in the funkhaus nalepastrasse berlin

kammerorchester berlin	lp: eterna 826 066
	cd: berlin classics 02682/91312

JOHANNES BRAHMS (1833-1897)
ein deutsches requiem op 45
recorded between 26-29 october 1957 in the funkhaus nalepastrasse berlin

rsob	lp: eterna 820 037-038
rundfunkchor berlin	
ebers, leib	

recorded between 5-11 february 1972 in the christuskirche

rsob	lp: eterna 826 318-319/deutsche
rundfunkchor berlin	schallplatten (japan) ET 4001-4002
tomova-sintow, leib	cd: berlin classics 30612

liebeslieder-walzer op 52
recorded between 25 january-6 february 1961 in the funkhaus nalepastrasse berlin

solistenvereinigung	lp: eterna 820 251/825 251
des deutschlandsenders	
vulpius, prenzlow,	
unger, leib,	
zechlin, kootz	

brahms/**neue liebeslieder-walzer op 65**
recorded between 25 january-6 february 1961 in the funkhaus
nalepastrasse berlin
solistenvereinigung   lp: eterna 820 251/825 251
des deutschlandsenders
vulpius, prenzlow,
unger, leib,
zechlin, kootz

**nachtwache I; nachtwache II/five songs for unaccompanied
chorus op 104**
recorded on 14 december 1957 in the funkhaus nalepastrasse berlin
solistenvereinigung   45: eterna 520 144
des deutschlandsenders   lp: eterna 820 251/825 251

HELMUT BRAEUTIGAM (1914-1942)
frühlingslied/five songs op 12
recorded on 28 february 1952 in the haus des rundfunks masurenallee berlin
solistenvereinigung   45: eterna 520 154
des deutschlandsenders

GIACOMO CARISSIMI (1605-1674)
jephte, oratorio
recorded on 1 november 1967 in the funkhaus nalepastrasse berlin
kammerorchester berlin   lp: eterna 826 076
rundfunkchor berlin
rönisch, woytowicz,
schreier

PETER CORNELIUS (1824-1874)
der tod das ist die kühle nacht/chorgesänge op 11
recorded on 14 december 1957 in the funkhaus nalepastrasse berlin
solistenvereinigung   45: eterna 520 144
des deutschlandsenders

HANNS EISLER (1898-1962)
cantata on the death of lenin (lenin-requiem 1937)
recorded between 27 november-22 december 1958 in the funkhaus
nalepastrasse berlin

rsob	45: eterna 520 233
rundfunkchor berlin	lp: eterna 860 154
solistenvereinigung	cd: berlin classics 90582
des deutschlandsenders	
arnold, hähnel	

neue deutsche volkslieder
recorded in october 1961 in the funkhaus nalepastrasse berlin

solistenvereinigung	lp: eterna 810 006/820 509/
des deutschlandsenders	825 509
vulpius, hübenthal,	*excerpts*
zechlin	lp: eterna 810 030
	cd: berlin classics 92322

lieder für kindergarten, to texts by brecht
recorded in october 1961 in the funkhaus nalepastrasse berlin

solistenvereingung	lp: eterna 810 006
des deutschlandsenders	cd: berlin classics 92322

nationalhymne der ddr (auferstanden aus ruinen)
national anthem of the german democratic republic

rsob	78: eterna 110 132
solistenvereinigung	45: eterna 410 117
des deutschlandsenders	lp: eterna 815 045
	cd: berlin classics 92322

nationalhymne der ddr, orchestral version
national anthem of the german democratic republic

rsob	78: eterna 110 132
	45: eterna 410 117
	lp: eterna 815 045

BALDASSARE GALUPPI (1706-1785)
se sapeste o giovinetti/l'amante di tutte
recorded between 30 may-6 june 1969 in the funkhaus nalepastrasse berlin

kammerorchester berlin	lp: eterna 826 074
schreier	cd: berlin classics 91852

FRANCESCO GASPARINI (1668-1727)
primavera che tutt' amorosa/importuno cupido
recorded between 30 may-6 june 1969 in the funkhaus nalepastrasse berlin
kammerorchester berlin   lp: eterna 826 074
schreier   cd: berlin classics 91392/91852

FRITZ GEISSLER (1921-1984)
schöpfer mensch, cantata
recorded between 3 march-30 may 1972 in the funkhaus nalepastrasse berlin
rsob   lp: eterna 885 044-045
rundfunkchor berlin
solistenvereinigung
des deutschlandsenders
schreier

FRANCESCO GEMINIANI (1687-1762)
concerto grosso op 3 no 1
recorded on 22 november 1968 in the funkhaus nalepastrasse berlin
kammerorchester berlin   lp: eterna 826 065/826 366
                             cd: berlin classics 30522/art 2988

OTTMAR GERSTER (1897-1969)
eisenhüttenkombinat ost, cantata
recorded between 3-5 september 1951 in the haus des rundfunks
masurenallee berlin
rsob   cd: hastedt HT 5311
rundfunkchor berlin
dresdner kreuzchor
oberschulchor
kleinmachnow
korch, kozub, rössler

CHRISTOPH WILLIBALD GLUCK (1714-1787)
die hochzeit von herkules und hebe
recorded between 6-10 april 1964 in the funkhaus nalepastrasse berlin
kammerorchester berlin   lp: eterna 820 677/825 677
vulpius, rönisch,   cd: berlin classics 91552
prenzlow, schreier   *recording completed in december 1966*

GEORGE FRIDERIC HANDEL (1685-1759)
music for the royal fireworks hwv351
recorded between 27 february-1 march 1974 in the funkhaus nalepastrasse

kammerorchester berlin   lp: eterna 826 809/deutsche
schallplatten (japan) ET 3043
cd: berlin classics 49482

water music, suite no 1 in f hwv348
recorded between 17-22 october 1969 in the funkhaus nalepastrasse berlin

kammerorchester berlin   lp: eterna 826 808/deutsche
schallplatten (japan) ET 3037
cd: berlin classics 49482

concerto grosso in d minor op 6 no 10 hwv328
recorded on 1-2 october 1957 in the funkhaus nalepastrasse berlin

kammerorchester berlin   lp: eterna 820 044

oboe concerto in g minor hwv287
recorded between 27 february-1 march 1974 in the funkhaus nalepastrasse

kammerorchester berlin   lp: eterna 826 809/deutsche
schallplatten (japan) ET 3043

violin concerto hwv288
recorded between 27 february-1 march 1974 in the funkhaus nalepastrasse

kammerorchester berlin   lp: eterna 826 809/deutsche
schallplatten (japan) ET 3043

dettinger te deum hwv283
recorded in september 1968 in the funkhaus nalepastrasse berlin

kammerorchester berlin   lp: eterna 825 971
solistenvereinigung   cd: berlin classics 93772
des deutschlandsenders
leib

ode for the birthday of queen anne hwv74/friedensode
recorded on 17 december 1957 in the funkhaus nalepastrasse berlin

kammerorchester berlin   lp: eterna 720 057
solistenvereinigung   *excerpts*
des deutschlandsenders   45: eterna 520 243
prenzlow, leib   lp: eterna 820 157/825 157
sung in german

handel/**acis and galatea, masque in two acts hwv49**
recorded in april 1959 in the funkhaus nalepastrasse berlin

kammerorchester berlin	lp: eterna 820 095-096/
solistenvereinigung	825 095-096
des deutschlandsenders	*excerpts*
vulpius, czerny,	45: eterna 520 272/520 279/
rotzsch, rössler	520 300
sung in german	lp: eterna 820 157/825 157

l'allegro il penseroso ed il moderato, ode in three parts hwv55
recorded between 3-28 may 1965 in the funkhaus nalepastrasse berlin

kammerorchester berlin	lp: eterna 825 539
solistenvereingung	*excerpts*
des deutschlandsenders	cd: art 3666
sung in german	

armida abandonata, solo cantata hwv105
recorded on 1 november 1967 in the funkhaus nalepastrasse berlin

kammerorchester berlin	lp: eterna 826 076
woytowicz	

belshazzar, oratorio hwv61/abridged version
recorded between 1950-1952 in the haus des rundfunks masurenallee berlin

rsob	lp: ducretet thomson 320C 003-005/
rundfunkchor berlin	vanguard BG 534-535/music
laux, müller, liebing,	treasures MTW 525-526
friedrich, alsen	
sung in german	

israel in egypt, oratorio hwv54
recorded between 1950-1952 in the haus des rundfunks masurenallee berlin

rsob	lp: vanguard BG 521-522/chant
rundfunkchor berlin	du monde LDX 8032-8033
bialas, welting, münzig,	
horst, räker, rungenhagen	
sung in german	

handel/**jephta, oratorio hwv70**
recorded between 22-30 april 1970 in the christuskirche

kammerorchester berlin   lp: eterna 826 189-191/
solistenvereinigung   eurodisc XGK 80541
des deutschlandsenders   *recording completed in june and october 1970*
stolte, burmeister,
prenzlow, schreier, adam
sung in german

judas maccabaeus, oratorio hwv63
recorded between 16-25 november 1966 in the funkhaus nalepastrasse berlin

rsob   lp: eterna 820 818-821/825 818-821/
rundfunkchor berlin   deutsche grammophon LPEM
solistenvereinigung   19 248-19 250/SLPEM 139 248-
des deutschlandsenders   139 250/2709 024
janowitz, töpper,   cd: berlin classics 32962/84692/
häfliger, schreier,   91122
adam, vogel   *excerpts*
sung in german   lp: eterna 820 701/820 822/825 822/
    deutsche grammophon 136 557
    cd: berlin classics 49482
    recording completed in january 1967

messiah, oratorio hwv56
recorded between 10-22 may 1958 in the funkhaus nalepastrasse berlin

rsob   lp: eterna 820 051-054/deutsche
rundfunkchor berlin   grammophon 2701 002/89 578-89 580/
wenglor, prenzlow,   muza (poland) XL 0084-0087
unger, adam   *excerpts*
sung in german   45: eterna 520 189/520 197/520 239
    lp: eterna 820 155/820 701

recorded in may-june 1973 in the funkhaus nalepastrasse berlin

rsob   lp: eterna 826 636-638/deutsche
rundfunkchor berlin   schallplatten (japan) ET 3017-3019
werner, riess,   cd: berlin classics 21242
schreier, adam   *excerpts*
sung in german   lp: eterna 826 617
    cd: berlin classics 49482/93812

handel/**semele, oratorio hwv58**
recorded in june 1974 in the funkhaus nalepastrasse berlin

rsob	lp: eterna/deutsche schallplatten
rundfunkchor berlin	(japan) ET 4006-4008
solistenvereinigung	cd: berlin classics 20902/84722
des deutschlandsenders	
hoff, werner, pohl,	
springer, büchner,	
lorenz, polster	

sung in german

JOHANN ADOLF HASSE (1699-1783)
tradir sapeste o perfidi/arminio
recorded between 30 may-6 june 1969 in the funkhaus nalepastrasse berlin

kammerorchester berlin	lp: eterna 826 074
schreier	cd: berlin classics 91852

FRANZ JOSEF HAYDN (1732-1809)
die schöpfung
recorded between 1950-1952 in the haus des rundfunks masurenallee berlin

rsob	lp: urania (usa) 235
rundfunkchor berlin	
korch, unger, adam	

recorded between 9-22 august 1960 in the funkhaus nalepastrasse berlin

rsob	lp: eterna 820 205-206/825 205-206/
rundfunkchor berlin	eurodisc XFK 80618/deutsche
solistenvereinigung	grammophon 89 576-89 577
des deutschlandsenders	*excerpts*
wenglor, unger, adam	lp: eterna 820 620/825 620/826 339/
	eurodisc 200 157.250

recorded between 28 january-9 february 1974 in the funkhaus
nalepastrasse berlin

rsob	lp: eterna 826 746-747/deutsche
rundfunkchor berlin	schallplatten (japan) ET 4011-4012
werner, riess	cd: berlin classics 91152
schreier, adam	*excerpts*
	cd: berlin classics 02042

haydn/**die jahreszeiten**
recorded between 10-13 october 1958 in the funkhaus nalepastrasse berlin

rsob	lp: eterna 820 040-042/deutsche
rundfunkchor berlin	schallplatten (japan) ET 3046-3047/
solistenvereinigung	ET 4009-4010/muza (poland)
des deutschlandsenders	XL 0089-0091
wenglor, unger, adam	*exerpts*
	45: eterna 520 234/520 235/520 342
	lp: eterna 820 620/826 339/860 082/
	philips fontana 697 017EL

missa in angustiis "nelson-messe"
recorded between 7-13 april 1971 in the funkhaus nalepastrasse berlin

rsob	lp: eterna 826 340/deutsche
solistenvereinigung	schallplatten (japan) CT 2018
des deutschlandsenders	cd: berlin classics 20912/32692
nawe, abrolat, prenzlow,	
reti, thomaschke	

piano concerto in d
recorded between 3-5 december 1958 in the funkhaus nalepastrasse berlin

kammerorchester berlin	lp: eterna 720 024
boschi	

trumpet concerto in e flat
recorded between 10-22 august 1970 in the funkhaus nalepastrasse berlin

kammerorchester berlin	lp: eterna 826 187
krug	cd: berlin classics 00362

PAUL HINDEMITH (1895-1963)
requiem for those we love
recorded on 1 january 1966 in the funkhaus nalepastrasse berlin

rsob	lp: eterna 825 832-833
solistenvereingung	cd: berlin classics 91702
des deutschlandsenders	
burmeister, leib	

WOLFGANG HOHENSEE (born 1927)
der schäfer vom hohen venn, cantata
recording date unspecified

rsob	unpublished radio broadcast
rundfunkchor berlin	*german radio archives*
vulpius, lauffer	

GUENTER KOCHAN (born 1932)
vier stücke für gemischten chor a capella: die republik;
lied vom drohnenkönig; wohl hab' ich oft und viel
gesungen; das hungerlied
recorded on 5 december 1961 in the funkhaus nalepastrasse berlin

solistenvereinigung	lp: eterna 825 884
des deutschlandsenders	*wohl hab' ich oft und viel gesungen*
	45: eterna 520 194
	recording completed in january 1962

SIEGFRIED KOEHLER (1927-1984)
reich des menschen, poem nach dichtungen von
johannes becher
recorded on 18 april 1966 in the funkhaus nalepastrasse berlin

rsob	lp: eterna 820 692/825 692
rundfunkchor berlin	*recording completed in may and october 1966*
solistenvereinigung	
des deutschlandsenders	
kuhse, prenzlow.	
schreier	

HEINZ KRAUSE-GRAUMNITZ
an die nachgeborenen, cantata
recorded on 1 october 1958 in the funkhaus nalepastrasse berlin
rsob   lp: eterna 710 019/825 884
rundfunkchor berlin
solistenvereinigung
des deutschlandsenders
prenzlow, apreck

weihnachtskantate nach worten von reiner kunze
recorded in september 1968 in the funkhaus nalepastrasse berlin
rsob   lp: eterna 825 992
solistenvereingung
des deutschlandsenders
czerny, prenzlow,
enders, frei

FRANZ LEHAR (1870-1948)
die lustige witwe, scenes from the operetta
recorded before 1945 in berlin
orchester des deutschen   unpublished radio broadcast
opernhauses   *german radio archives*
rose, jautz

**wolgalied/der zarewitsch; immer nur lächeln/das land
des lächelns**
recorded before 1945 in berlin
orchester des deutschen   unpublished radio broadcast
opernhauses   *german radio archives*
jautz

LEONARDO LEO (1694-1744)
son qual nave in ria procella/zenobia in palmira
recorded between 30 may-6 june 1969 in the funkhaus nalepastrasse berlin
kammerorchester berlin   lp: eterna 826 074
schreier   cd: berlin classics 91852

PIETRO ANTONIO LOCATELLI (1695-1764)
concerto grosso in f op 7 no 12
recorded on 1-2 november 1968 in the funkhaus nalepastrasse berlin
kammerorchester berlin   lp: eterna 826 065/826 366
cd: berlin classics 30522/art 3666

BENEDETTO MARCELLO (1686-1739)
latte e miele ecco veggio/arianna
recorded between 30 may-6 june 1969 in the funkhaus nalepastrasse berlin
kammerorchester berlin   lp: eterna 826 074
schreier   cd: berlin classics 91852

col pianto e coi sospiri, aria
recorded between 30 may-6 june 1969 in the funkhaus nalepastrasse berlin
kammerorchester berlin   lp: eterna 826 074
schreier   cd: berlin classics 91852

FELIX MENDELSSOHN-BARTHOLDY (1809-1847)
violin concerto in d minor
recorded on 1 october 1972 in the christuskirche
kammerorchester berlin   lp: eterna 826 347
schmahl   cd: berlin classics 00692/30892

ERNST HERMANN MEYER (1905-1988)

mansfelder oratorium

commissioned for the seven hundred and fiftieth anniversary of
the mansfeld copper mine near halle

recorded between 3-9 december 1956 in berlin

rsob	lp: eterna 710 051-053/825 871-872
rundfunkchor berlin	*excerpts*
solistenvereinigung	45: eterna 510 008/520 172/
des deutschlandsenders	520 173/520 174
prenzlow, trösch, leib	

des sieges gewissheit, cantata

recorded between 16-19 july 1953 in the bergmann-borsig-kultursaal

rsob	unpublished radio broadcast
solistenvereingung	*excerpts*
des deutschlandsenders	78: eterna 110 249
wall-lade, drews,	45: eterna 510 008
kozub	lp: eterna 810 022/820 509

nachtlied/landschaftsbilder aus deutschland

recorded on 28 february 1952 in the funkhaus nalepastrasse berlin

solistenvereinigung	45: eterna 520 154
des deutschlandsenders	

concerto grosso for timpani and strings

recorded between 10-13 march 1967 in the funkhaus nalepastrasse berlin

kammerorchester berlin	lp: eterna 825 985

harp concerto

recorded between 9-19 february 1969 in the funkhaus nalepastrasse berlin

kammerorchester berlin	lp: eterna 825 985

CLAUDIO MONTEVERDI (1567-1643)
l'orfeo, favola in musica
recorded between 18 november-6 december 1949 in the haus des rundfunks
masurenallee berlin

kammerorchester berlin	lp: eterna 820 036-038/discophile
solistenvereinigung	francais DF 4244/vox PL 6443/VBX 21
des deutschlandsenders	cd: berlin classics 94342/cantus
trötschel, lammers,	classics 500 422
krebs, meili, kahl	

sung in german

ecco pur ch'a voi ritorno/l'orfeo
recorded between 30 may-6 june 1969 in the funkhaus nalepastrasse berlin

kammerorchester berlin	lp: eterna 826 074
schreier	cd: berlin classics 91392/91852

vespro della beata vergine
recorded in december 1967 in the funkhaus nalepastrasse berlin

kammerorchester berlin	lp: eterna 826 086-087
solistenvereinigung	*may also have been published on cd by*
des deutschlandsenders	*denon in japan*

LEOPOLD MOZART (1719-1787)
die bauernhochzeit, sinfonia
recorded between 2-4 june 1969 in the studio brunnenstrasse berlin

kammerorchester berlin	lp: eterna 825 670
	cd: berlin classics 30142

kindersinfonie/from cassation in g
recorded between 2-4 june 1969 in the studio brunnenstrasse berlin

kammerorchester berlin	lp: eterna 825 670
	cd: berlin classics 30142/art 3866

trumpet concerto
recorded between 10-22 august 1970 in the funkhaus nalepastrasse berlin

kammerorchester berlin	lp: eterna 826 187
krug	cd: berlin classics 00362

a live broadcast performance with the same soloist may have been
published by wea and pilz acanta

musikalische schlittenfahrt
recorded between 2-4 june 1969 in the studio brunnenstrasse berlin

kammerorchester berlin	lp: eterna 825 670
	cd: berlin classics 30142/
	art 4385/3866

WOLFGANG AMADEUS MOZART (1756-1791)
serenade no 4 in d k203
recorded between 26-29 november 1964 in the funkhaus nalepastrasse berlin

kammerorchester berlin   unpublished radio broadcast
german radio archives

serenade no 5 in d k204
recorded on 2 march 1969 in the funkhaus nalepastrasse berlin

kammerorchester berlin   unpublished radio broadcast
german radio archives

flute concerto in d k314
recorded on 13 december 1969 in the funkhaus nalepastrasse berlin

kammerorchester berlin   unpublished radio broadcast
wätzig   *german radio archives*

march in d k215
recorded on 2 march 1969 in the funkhaus nalepastrasse berlin

kammerorchester berlin   unpublished radio broadcast
german radio archives

march in d k249
recorded on 13 december 1966 in the funkhaus nalepastrasse berlin

kammerorchester berlin   unpublished radio broadcast
german radio archives

three marches in d k408
recorded on 13 december 1966 in the funkhaus nalepastrasse berlin

kammerorchester berlin   unpublished radio broadcast
german radio archives

four church sonatas for organ and strings k224, k225, k244 and k245
recorded on 25 june 1967 in the funkhaus nalepastrasse nerlin

kammerorchester berlin   unpublished radio broadcast
köbler   *german radio archives*

mozart/mass in c minor k427 "great"
recorded between 6-10 january 1964 in the funkhaus nalepastrasse berlin

rsob	lp: eterna 820 404-406/825 404-406/
solistenvereinigung	eurodisc XAK 27820
des deutschlandsenders	cd: berlin classics 02112
czerny, wenglor,	*recording completed in april 1964*
apreck, adam	

requiem in d minor k626
recorded between 26-30 november 1962 in the funkhaus nalepastrasse berlin

rsob	lp: eterna 820 404-406/825 404-406
solistenvereinigung	cd: berlin classics 31062
des deutschlandsenders	
vulpius, prenzlow,	
apreck, adam	

dir seele des weltalls, cantata k429
recorded on 3 october 1963 in the funkhaus nalepastrasse berlin

rsob	unpublished radio broadcast
solistenvereinigung	*german radio archives*
des deutschlandsenders	

recorded on 22 may 1967 at a concert in the metropoltheater berlin

rsob	unpublished radio broadcast
solistenvereinigung	*german radio archives*
des deutschlandsenders	

misero o sogno, concert aria k431
recorded in november 1968 in the christuskirche

kammerorchester berlin	cd: berlin classics 91292
schreier	*unpublished eterna lp recording*

per pieta non ricercato, concert aria k420
recorded in november 1968 in the christuskirche

kammerorchester berlin	lp: eterna 826 073
schreier	cd: berlin classics 91292

bastien und bastienne, singspiel k50
recorded between 21-27 july 1965 in the funkhaus nalepastrasse berlin

kammerorchester berlin	lp: eterna 820 661/825 661/
stolte, schreier, adam	deutsche grammophon SLPEM
	139 213-139 215/2705 005/
	2709 021
	cd: berlin classics 91292

mozart/**deh per questo istante solo/la clemenza di tito**
recorded on 18 june 1964 in the funkhaus nalepastrasse berlin
rsob   unpublished radio broadcast
i.ludwig   *german radio archives*
sung in german

der schauspieldirektor k486
recorded between 4-8 february 1968 in the christuskirche
kammerorchester berlin   lp: eterna 826 073
geszty, schreier, polster   cd: berlin classics 32602/91362/
                                              brilliant classics 99723-4
                                              recording completed between november 1968-
                                              january 1969

thamos könig von ägypten, incidental music to the play
recorded on 27-28 june 1963 in the funkhaus nalepastrasse berlin
rsob   unpublished radio broadcast
solistenvereinigung   *german radio archives*
des deutschlandsenders
stolte, schriever,
neukirch, hausmann

PIETRO NARDINI (1722-1793)
violin concerto in e minor
recorded between 25-29 may 1970 in the christuskirche
kammerorchester berlin   lp: eterna 826 180
scherzer   cd: berlin classics 31952
                                              recording completed in december 1970

GIOVANNI BATTISTA PERGOLESI (1710-1736)
la serva padrona, opera buffa
recorded on 13 july 1970 in the christuskirche
staatskapelle berlin   lp: eterna 826 201/telefunken
miljakovic, süss   SLT 43126
sung in german   cd: berlin classics 91142
                                              recording completed in december 1970

pergolesi/**six concertini for strings**
recorded between 7-20 october 1965 in the funkhaus nalepastrasse berlin
kammercrchester berlin   lp: eterna 820 702-703/825 702-703
                                              excerpts
                                              lp: philips fontana grandioso
                                              894 045ZKY
                                              recordings completed between november 1965-
                                              june 1966

flute concerto in g
recorded between 7-20 october 1965 in the funkhaus nalepastrasse berlin
kammerorchester berlin   lp: eterna 820 702-703/825 702-703
walter

BELA REINITZ (1878-1943)
bundeslied für den allgemeinen deutschen arbeiterverein
recording date unspecified
bläsergruppe und   lp: eterna
männerchor der
komischen oper berlin

ALESSANDRO SCARLATTI (1660-1725)
sinfonia no 2 in d
recorded on 24 october 1968 in the funkhaus nalepastrasse berlin
kammerorchester berlin   lp: eterna 826 065/826 366
                                              cd: berlin classics 30522

rugiadose odorose violette graziose/il pirro e demeluo
recorded between 30 may-6 june 1969 in the funkhaus nalepastrasse berlin
kammerorchester berlin   lp: eterna 826 074
schreier   cd: berlin classics 91852

ARNOLD SCHOENBERG (1874-1951)
friede auf erden op 13
recording date unspecified
solistenvereinigung   lp: eterna 820 201/825 201
des deutschlandsenders

FRANZ SCHUBERT (1797-1828)
deutsche messe d872
recording date unspecified
rsob   unpublished radio broadcast
rundfunkchor berlin   *german radio archives*

HEINRICH SCHUETZ (1585-1672)
matthäus-passion
recorded between 1950-1952 in the haus des rundfunks masurenallee berlin
solistenvereinigung   lp: vanguard BG 519-520/chant
des deutschlandsenders   du monde LDX 8029-8030
meili, rüngenhausen,
michaelis, wilhelm,
patzke, räker

LEO SPIES (1889-1965)
lasst uns zusammen gehen
recording date unspecified
solistenvereinigung   lp: eterna 820 509/825 509
des deutschlandsenders

CARL STAMITZ (1745-1801)
cello concerto/unspecified
recording date unspecified
kammerorchester berlin   cd: pilz acanta 44 20792
zimmermann

ANGELO STEFFANI (1654-1728)
a facile vittoria; piangerete io ben lo so/tassilone
recorded between 30 may-6 june 1969 in the funkhaus nalepastrasse berlin
kammerorchester berlin   lp: eterna 826 074
schreier   cd: berlin classics 91852

GEORG PHILIPP TELEMANN (1681-1767)
pimpione, oder die ungleiche heirat
recorded on 31 march 1964 in the christuskirche

staatskapelle berlin   lp: eterna 820 459/825 459/
röscher, süss   philips 9502 117
                                   cd: berlin classics 20712
                                   recording completed in april 1964

ino, solo cantata
recorded on 10-11 september 1969 in the christuskirche

kammerorchester berlin   lp: eterna 826 078
stolte   cd: berlin classics 01452
                                   recording completed in october 1969

die tageszeiten, cantata
recorded between 21-23 february 1958 in the funkhaus nalepastrasse berlin

kammerorchester berlin   lp: eterna 820 301/825 301
solistenvereinigung
des deutschlandsenders
czerny, prenzlow,
unger, leib

non ho piu core/der geduldige sokrates
recorded between 30 may-6 june 1969 in the funkhaus nalepastrasse berlin

kammerorchester berlin   lp: eterna 826 074
schreier   cd: berlin classics 91852

trumpet concerto in d
recorded between 10-22 august 1970 in the funkhaus nalepastrasse berlin

kammerorchester berlin   lp: eterna 826 187
krug   cd: berlin classics 00362

overture in b flat/tafelmusik III
recorded in 1961-1962 in the funkhaus nalepastrasse berlin

kammerorchester berlin   lp: eterna 820 264/825 264/
                                   deutsche grammophon 89 543
                                   cd: berlin classics 01912/31752/
                                   art 3666/5969

overture in g minor
recorded in 1969 in the funkhaus nalepastrasse berlin

kammerorchester berlin   lp: eterna 825 982

telemann/**triple concerto in e**
recorded in 1961-1962 in the funkhaus nalepastrasse berlin

kammerorchester berlin	lp: eterna 820 264/825 264/
milzkott, fricke, wätzke	deutsche grammophon 89 543
	cd: berlin classics 31752

trio sonata in c minor
recorded in 1961-1962 in the funkhaus nalepastrasse berlin

kammerorchester berlin	lp: eterna 820 264/825 264/
	deutsche grammophon 89 543

GIUSEPPE TORELLI (1658-1709)
trumpet concerto in d
recorded between 10-22 august 1970 in the funkhaus nalepastrasse berlin

kammerorchester berlin	lp: eterna 826 187
krug	cd: berlin classics 00362/30522/
	art 4393

GIUSEPPE VERDI (1813-1901)
messa da requiem
recorded in 1962 at a concert in berlin

rsob	unpublished radio broadcast
rundfunkchor berlin	*german radio archives*
solistenvereinigung	
des deutschlandsenders	
wiener, prenzlow,	
schreier, adam	

unpublished verdi arias, choruses and ballet music may also survive in german radio archives

GIOVANNI BATTISTA VIOTTI (1755-1824)
violin concerto no 22 in a minor
recorded between 25-29 may 1970 in the funkhaus nalepastrasse berlin

kammerorchester berlin	lp: eterna 826 180
scherzer	cd: berlin classics 31952
	recording completed in december 1970

ANTONIO VIVALDI (1678-1741)
violin concerto in a minor rv356
recored between 25-29 may 1970 in the funkhaus nalepastrasse berlin
kammerorchester berlin   lp: eterna 826 180
scherzer   cd: berlin classics 01942/30362/
                          31952/art 3613/3693/3929
                          recording completed in december 1970
bassoon concerto in d minor rv481
recorded on 14 december 1969 in the funkhaus nalepastrasse berlin
kammerorchester berlin   lp: eterna 826 065/826 366
pischkitl   cd: berlin classics 01942/30522
piccolo concerto in c rv443
recorded on 4 november 1969 in the funkhaus nalepastrasse berlin
kammerorchester berlin   lp: eterna 826 065/826 366
tast   cd: berlin classics 01942/30522

WILHELM WEISMANN (1900-1980)
liebeslieder nach gedichten des 12. jahrhunderts; madrigale
nach worten von hölderlin; der neue tristan
recorded between august 1967-january 1968
solistenvereinigung   lp: eterna 825 919
des deutschlandsenders

RUTH ZECHLIN (born 1926)
wenn der wachholder wieder blüht, oratorio
recorded in july 1960 in the funkhaus nalepastrasse berlin
rundfunkchor berlin   lp: eterna 820 216/825 216
solistenvereinigung
des deutschlandsenders
vulpius, cervena,
apreck, süss
lidice cantata
recorded in october 1961 in the funkhaus nalepastrasse berlin
rsob   lp: eterna 720 080
solistenvereingung
des deutschlandsenders
kögel
kammersinfonie
recorded in 1972 in the funkhaus nalepastrasse berlin
kammerorchester berlin   lp: eterna 885 026

MISCELLANEOUS

musikalische eulenspiegelein/humour in music
works include eskapaden eines gassenhauers
recorded in november 1967 in the funkhaus nalepastrasse berlin
kammerorchester berlin   lp: eterna 826 017

deutsche, italienische und englische madrigale
recorded in 1962 in berlin
solistenvereinigung   lp: eterna 830 004/835 004
des deutschlandsenders

**das deutsche chorlied I: madrigale aus dem 16. und 17.
jahrhundert**
recorded in 1963 in berlin
solistenvereinigung   lp: eterna 830 007/835 007
des deutschlansenders

**das deutsche chorlied II: madrigale aus dem 18. und 19.
jahrhundert**
recorded in 1964 in berlin
solistenvereinigung   lp: eterna 830 020/835 020
des deutschlandsenders

deutsche lieder mit arien des 17. jahrhunderts
recorded between 23-26 november 1970 in the versöhnungskirche leipzig
solistenvereinigung   lp: eterna 826 311
des deutschlandsenders   *recording completed in may 1971*

christmas carols
recorded between 1955-1957 in berlin
solistenvereinigung   78: eterna 120 200/120 201/120 206
des deutschlandsenders   45: eterna 520 031/520 032

index of instrumental soloists who feature in these discographies

instrumental soloists/concluded

manfred reinelt/piano
werner richter/piano
heinz rögner/piano
rüpular/clarinet

magdalena rezler/violin
hans richter-haaser/piano
peter rösel/piano

jakow sak/piano
günter schaffrath/horn
heinrich schiff/cello
annerose schmidt/piano
renate schorler/piano
manfred schumann/violin
karl schütte/clarinet
wolfgang stephan/trumpet
karl suske/violin

natalia schachowskaja/cello
manfred scherzer/violin
gustav schmahl/violin
fritz schneider/oboe
karl-heinz schröter/cello
heinz schunk/violin
sergei stadler/violin
siegfried stöckigt/piano

werner tast/piccolo
alfred tolksdorf/oboe
viktor tretjakow/violin

jürnjakob timm/cello
paul tortelier/cello

uhse/piano

maria vermes/violin

ion voicu/violin

johannes walter/flute
hans-werner wätzig/oboe
amadeus webersinke/organ
antje weithaas/violin

heinz wappler/bassoon
amadeus webersinke/piano
sebastian weigle/horn
wanda wilmomirska/violin

dieter zechlin/piano
jutta zoff/harp

zimmermann/cello

index of vocal soloists who feature in these discographies
includes singers who appeared in recordings made outside the ddr

abrolat/soprano

wolf appel/tenor

elisabeth aldor/soprano

irmgard arnold/soprano

theo adam/bass-baritone

rolf apreck/tenor

herbert alsen/bass

aldo baldin/tenor

barmeli/bass

bauer/mezzo

bialas/mezzo

kurt böhme/bass

philip booth/baritone

eberhard büchner/tenor

reid bunger/bass

bardini/tenor

olaf bär/baritone

walter berry/bass

peter bindszus/tenor

els bolkestein/soprano

elisabeth breul/soprano

eva maria bundschuh/soprano

annelies burmeister/mezzo

celestina casapietra/soprano

sona cervena/contralto

cittanti/bass

franz crass/bass

ingrid czerny/soprano

nedda casei/mezzo

lili chookasian/contralto

ulrich cold/bass

maria croonen/soprano

gloria davy/mezzo

william dooley/baritone

ludmila dvorakova/soprano

helen donath/soprano

marianne drews/soprano

clara ebers/soprano

brigitte eisenfeld/soprano

werner enders/tenor

siw eriksdotter/mezzo

hermin esser/tenor

geraint evans/bass-baritone

elisabeth ebert/soprano

emmerlich/baritone

barbro ericson/mezzo

esching/tenor

diana eustrati/contralto

magdalena falewicz/soprano

ezio flagello/bass

jürgen förster/tenor

gerhard frei/bass

brünnhilde friedland/soprano

dietrich fischer-dieskau/baritone

eva fleischer/contralto

renate frank-reinecke/soprano

venzeslava rhuba-freiberger/soprano

heinz friedrich/baritone

vocal soloists/continued

else-margret gardelli/soprano
nicolai gedda/tenor
reiner goldberg/tenor
jill gomez/soprano
ernst gruber/tenor
ernst gutstein/bass-baritone

henno garduhn/tenor
sylvia geszty/soprano
christel goltz/soprano
clifford grant/bass
peter van gunkel/bass

ernst haefliger/tenor
margarete hahnkamm/mezzo
magdalena hajossyova/soprano
alison hargan/soprano
hauchwitz/contralto
uwe heilmann/tenor
horst hiestermann/tenor
irma hofer/soprano
marga höffgen/contralto
karl heinz hölzke/tenor
heinz hoppe/tenor
wilhelm horst/tenor
fritz hübner/bass-baritone

ann-marie häggander/soprano
hermann hähnel/baritone
ingeborg hallstein/soprano
werner haseleu/baritone
siegfried hausmann/bass
wolfgang hellmich/baritone
klaus hirte/tenor
renate hoff/soprano
hubert hofmann/bass-baritone
hans hopf/tenor
theodor horand/bass
kurt hübenthal/baritone

krystyna jamroz/soprano
karl jautz/tenor
manfred jungwirth/bass

gundula janowitz/soprano
manfred jung/tenor

hilbert kahl/bass
hannelore katterfeld/contralto
hans-joachim ketelsen/baritone
klamm/tenor
rene kollo/tenor
györgy korondi/tenor
ernst kozub/tenor
gunter krämer/baritone
rolf kühne/bass-baritone
hannelore kuhse/soprano

helmut kapphahn/bass
sigrid kehl/contralto
james king/tenor
kurt kögel/baritonr
sonja-vera korch/soprano
kolos kovats/bass
renate krahmer/soprano
helmut krebs/tenor
kühnert/tenor
jürgen kurth/baritone

vocal soloists/continued
peter lagger/bass
lampe/soprano
rosemarie lang/contralto
robert lauhöfer/baritone
günter leib/bass-baritone
catarina ligendza/soprano
berit lindholm/soprano
hans löbel/baritone
kari lövaas/soprano
ralf ludwig/speaker
horst lunow/bass

violetta madjarova/mezzo
regina marheineke/soprano
edith mathis/soprano
franz mazura/bass-baritone
helmut melchert/tenor
arnold van mill/bass
kurt moll/bass
annelies müller/contralto
hedwig müller-bütow/soprano

ann-katrin naidu/mezzo
günter naumann/bass
gustav neidlinger/bass-baritone
harald neukirch/tenor
wolfgang neumann/tenor
birgit nilsson/soprano
carola nossek/soprano

johann oettel/bass
fritz ollendorff/bass
sigune von osten/soprano

gerd pallesche/baritone
petorsek/soprano
gisela pohl/mezzo
hermann prey/baritone
uta priew/mezzo
ruth margret pütz/soprano

gerda lammers/soprano
landucci/soprano
sergei larin/tenor
elisabeth laux/soprano
werner liebing/tenor
margarita lilowa/contralto
gisela litz/mezzo
siegfried lorenz/baritone
ilse ludwig/contralto
rainer lüdeke/bass
gerd lutze/tenor

annette maikert/soprano
janis martin/soprano
gisela may/soprano
max meili/tenor
oliviera miljakovic/soprano
alexander miltschinoff/tenor
morgan/mezzo
hajo müller/bass
münzing/mezzo

marita napier/soprano
isabelle nawe/soprano
evgeny nesterenko/bass
günter neumann/tenor
gerd nienstedt/baritone
siegmund nimsgern/baritone

peter olesch/tenor
william olvis/tenor
luba orgonasova/soprano

patzke/baritone
walter pietsch/bass
hermann christian polster/bass
gertraud prenzlow/contralto
ana pusar/soprano

vocal soloists/continued
räker/baritone
jadwiga rappe/contralto
david rendall/tenor
hans joachim ribbe/bass
karl ridderbusch/bass
heidi riess/mezzo
martin ritzmann/tenor
anthony roden/tenor
erna röscher/soprano
herbert rössler/bass
annelise rothenberger/soprano
hans joachim rotzsch/tenor
leonie rysanek/soprano

eva randova/mezzo
ursula reinhardt-kiss/soprano
josef reti/tenor
ursula richter/soprano
bernd riedl/baritone
rist/soprano
stephen roberts/baritone
rosemarie rönisch/soprano
elisabeth rose/soprano
peter roth-ehrang/bass
helena rott/contralto
rüngenhagen/bass
lotte rysanek/soprano

arleen saunders/soprano
alfred schelske/baritone
marga schiml/contralto
andreas schmidt/baritone
sonja schöner/soprano
gisela schröter/mezzo
horst schulze/speaker
hanna schwarz/mezzo
kurt schüffler/tenor
amy shuard/soprano
vera soukupova/contralto
thomas stewart/bass-baritone
adele stolte/soprano
karl heinz stryczek/baritone
antonin svorc/baritone

dagmar schellenberger/soprano
manfred schenk/bass
anny schlemm/soprano
peter jürgen schmidt/tenor
peter schreier/tenor
annelies schubert-heuhaus/soprano
dieter schwartner/tenor
schwerdegger/bass
arturo sergi/tenor
anja silja/soprano
ingeborg springer/contralto
gertrud stilo/mezzo
gerhard stolze/tenor
reiner süss/bass

vocal soloists/concluded
martti talvela/bass
fred teschler/baritone
thomas thomaschke/bass
anna tomova-sintow/soprano
giorgio tozzi/bass
ute trekel-burkhardt/mezzo
elfride trötschel/soprano

armin ude/tenor
gerhard unger/tenor

helen vanni/soprano
christian vogel/tenor
silvia voinea/soprano

eberhard wächter/baritone
ingeborg wall-lade/soprano
dieter weimann/tenor
spas wenkoff/tenor
westmayer/baritone
horst wilhelm/bass
hermann winkler/tenor
hans wocke/baritone
karl wolfram/baritone

bernd zettisch/bass

helga termer/soprano
jess thomas/tenor
tinschert/tenor
hertha töpper/contralto
roman trekel/baritone
roswitha trexler/soprano

ragnar ulfung/tenor

astrid varnay/soprano
siegfried vogel/bass
jutta vulpius/soprano

john edward walker/tenor
ute walther/contralto
ingeborg wenglor/soprano
regina werner/soprano
gerd westphal/speaker
wolfgang windgassen/tenor
ekkehard wlaschiha/bass
erwin wohlfahrt/tenor
stefania woytowicz/soprano

christa maria ziese/soprano

list of subscribers

production of these discographies would not have been possible without the loyal support of

Yoshihiro Asada
Philip Goodman
Detlef Kissmann
Carlo Marinelli
Yoshihiko Suzuki

Richard Ames
Reinier van Bevervoorde
Michael Bral
Brian Capon
Dennis Davis
Hans Peter Ebner
Peter Fülop
Johann Gratz
Tadashi Hasegawa
E.M. Johnson
Koji Kinoshita
Graham Lilley
Philip Moores
William Moyle
Gregory Page-Turner
David Patmore
J.A. Payne
Tully Potter
Yutaka Sasaki
Robert Simmons
Nigel Wood
Ken Wyman

John Derry
Jean-Pierre Goossens
Douglas McIntosh
Laurence Pateman
Urs Weber

Stefano Angeloni
J.M. Blyth
Marc Bridle
Robert Dandois
Richard Dennis
Nobuo Fukumoto
Brian Godfrey
Alan Haine
Naoya Hirabayashi
Rodney Kempster
J-F. Lambert
John Mallinson
Bruce Morrison
Alan Newcombe
Hugh Palmer
John Pattrick
James Pearson
Klaus Reuther
Ingo Schwarz
Michael Tanner
Graeme Wright

Discographies by Travis & Emery:

Discographies by John Hunt.

1987: From Adam to Webern: the Recordings of von Karajan.
1991: 3 Italian Conductors and 7 Viennese Sopranos: 10 Discographies: Arturo Toscanini, Guido Cantelli, Carlo Maria Giulini, Elisabeth Schwarzkopf, Irmgard Seefried, Elisabeth Gruemmer, Sena Jurinac, Hilde Gueden, Lisa Della Casa, Rita Streich.
1992: Mid-Century Conductors and More Viennese Singers: 10 Discographies: Karl Boehm, Victor De Sabata, Hans Knappertsbusch, Tullio Serafin, Clemens Krauss, Anton Dermota, Leonie Rysanek, Eberhard Waechter, Maria Reining, Erich Kunz.
1993: More 20th Century Conductors: 7 Discographies: Eugen Jochum, Ferenc Fricsay, Carl Schuricht, Felix Weingartner, Josef Krips, Otto Klemperer, Erich Kleiber.
1994: Giants of the Keyboard: 6 Discographies: Wilhelm Kempff, Walter Gieseking, Edwin Fischer, Clara Haskil, Wilhelm Backhaus, Artur Schnabel.
1994: Six Wagnerian Sopranos: 6 Discographies: Frieda Leider, Kirsten Flagstad, Astrid Varnay, Martha Moedl, Birgit Nilsson, Gwyneth Jones.
1995: Musical Knights: 6 Discographies: Henry Wood, Thomas Beecham, Adrian Boult, John Barbirolli, Reginald Goodall, Malcolm Sargent.
1995: A Notable Quartet: 4 Discographies: Gundula Janowitz, Christa Ludwig, Nicolai Gedda, Dietrich Fischer-Dieskau.
1996: The Post-War German Tradition: 5 Discographies: Rudolf Kempe, Joseph Keilberth, Wolfgang Sawallisch, Rafael Kubelik, Andre Cluytens.
1996: Teachers and Pupils: 7 Discographies: Elisabeth Schwarzkopf, Maria Ivoguen, Maria Cebotari, Meta Seinemeyer, Ljuba Welitsch, Rita Streich, Erna Berger.
1996: Tenors in a Lyric Tradition: 3 Discographies: Peter Anders, Walther Ludwig, Fritz Wunderlich.
1997: The Lyric Baritone: 5 Discographies: Hans Reinmar, Gerhard Hüsch, Josef Metternich, Hermann Uhde, Eberhard Wächter.
1997: Hungarians in Exile: 3 Discographies: Fritz Reiner, Antal Dorati, George Szell.
1997: The Art of the Diva: 3 Discographies: Claudia Muzio, Maria Callas, Magda Olivero.
1997: Metropolitan Sopranos: 4 Discographies: Rosa Ponselle, Eleanor Steber, Zinka Milanov, Leontyne Price.
1997: Back From The Shadows: 4 Discographies: Willem Mengelberg, Dimitri Mitropoulos, Hermann Abendroth, Eduard Van Beinum.
1997: More Musical Knights: 4 Discographies: Hamilton Harty, Charles Mackerras, Simon Rattle, John Pritchard.
1998: Conductors On The Yellow Label: 8 Discographies: Fritz Lehmann, Ferdinand Leitner, Ferenc Fricsay, Eugen Jochum, Leopold Ludwig, Artur Rother, Franz Konwitschny, Igor Markevitch.
1998: More Giants of the Keyboard: 5 Discographies: Claudio Arrau, Gyorgy Cziffra, Vladimir Horowitz, Dinu Lipatti, Artur Rubinstein.

1998: Mezzos and Contraltos: 5 Discographies: Janet Baker, Margarete Klose, Kathleen Ferrier, Giulietta Simionato, Elisabeth Höngen.

1999: The Furtwängler Sound Sixth Edition: Discography and Concert Listing.

1999: The Great Dictators: 3 Discographies: Evgeny Mravinsky, Artur Rodzinski, Sergiu Celibidache.

1999: Sviatoslav Richter: Pianist of the Century: Discography.

2000: Philharmonic Autocrat 1: Discography of: Herbert Von Karajan [Third Edition].

2000: Wiener Philharmoniker 1 - Vienna Philharmonic & Vienna State Opera Orchestras: Disc. Part 1 1905-1954.

2000: Wiener Philharmoniker 2 - Vienna Philharmonic & Vienna State Opera Orchestras: Disc. Part 2 1954-1989.

2001: Gramophone Stalwarts: 3 Separate Discographies: Bruno Walter, Erich Leinsdorf, Georg Solti.

2001: Singers of the Third Reich: 5 Discographies: Helge Roswaenge, Tiana Lemnitz, Franz Völker, Maria Müller, Max Lorenz.

2001: Philharmonic Autocrat 2: Concert Register of Herbert Von Karajan Second Edition.

2002: Sächsische Staatskapelle Dresden: Complete Discography.

2002: Carlo Maria Giulini: Discography and Concert Register.

2002: Pianists For The Connoisseur: 6 Discographies: Arturo Benedetti Michelangeli, Alfred Cortot, Alexis Weissenberg, Clifford Curzon, Solomon, Elly Ney.

2003: Singers on the Yellow Label: 7 Discographies: Maria Stader, Elfriede Trötschel, Annelies Kupper, Wolfgang Windgassen, Ernst Häfliger, Josef Greindl, Kim Borg.

2003: A Gallic Trio: 3 Discographies: Charles Münch, Paul Paray, Pierre Monteux.

2004: Antal Dorati 1906-1988: Discography and Concert Register.

2004: Columbia 33CX Label Discography.

2004: Great Violinists: 3 Discographies: David Oistrakh, Wolfgang Schneiderhan, Arthur Grumiaux.

2006: Leopold Stokowski: Second Edition of the Discography.

2006: Wagner Im Festspielhaus: Discography of the Bayreuth Festival.

2006: Her Master's Voice: Concert Register and Discography of Dame Elisabeth Schwarzkopf [Third Edition].

2007: Hans Knappertsbusch: Kna: Concert Register and Discography of Hans Knappertsbusch, 1888-1965. Second Edition.

2008: Philips Minigroove: Second Extended Version of the European Discography.

2009: American Classics: The Discographies of Leonard Bernstein and Eugene Ormandy.

2010: Dirigenten der DDR. Conductors of the German Democratic Republic. Otmar Suitner, Herbert Kegel, Heinz Rögner (Rogner), Heinz Bongartz and Helmut Koch.

Discography by Stephen J. Pettitt, edited by John Hunt:

1987: Philharmonia Orchestra: Complete Discography 1945-1987

Available from: Travis & Emery at 17 Cecil Court, London, UK.
(+44) 20 7 240 2129. email on sales@travis-and-emery.com .

Lightning Source UK Ltd.
Milton Keynes UK
UKOW030718110212

187097UK00001B/56/P